Instead of giving young people the impression
that their task is to stand in dreary watch
over the ancient values,
we should be telling them the grim but bracing truth
that it is their task continually to recreate those values
in their own behavior, facing the dilemmas and catastrophies
of their own time.
Instead of implying that the ideals we cherish are safely
embalmed in the memory of old battles and ancestral deeds,
we should be telling them that each generation refights
the crucial battles and either brings new vitality
to the ideals
or allows them to decay . . .

John W. Gardner

VALUES EDUCATION SERIES
McDougal, Littell & Company • Evanston, Illinois

DECIDING HOW TO ACT IN A POLITICAL SOCIETY

THE ETHICS OF POLITICAL BEHAVIOR

by
John E. Boland
Charles J. O'Fahey
Darryll L. Olson

Sheila Moriarty O'Fahey, editor

Ulric C. Scott, consultant

Acknowledgments: See page 122

Photo credits: See page 122

ISBN 0-88343-673-6

Library of Congress Card Catalog # 75-9169

Published 1975 by McDougal, Littell & Company
Box 1667, Evanston, Illinois.
Copyright © 1975 by St. Mary's College Press, Winona, Minnesota

CONTENTS

ENCOUNTERS WITH CHOICE

"**Whenever a sufficient number of voters act in unison there is no legal limit to their power. They reign in the American political world as God does in the universe.**"

Alexis de Tocqueville

As we move into the two hundredth anniversary of our country, many Americans wonder about the validity of de Tocqueville's statement. They are asking deep, searching questions about the political system. Apathy, cynicism, and indignation characterize the attitudes of some citizens. Many others do not believe they can affect the political system. If we are to preserve the democratic ideal of representative government upon which our country was founded, we need to correct this perspective.

Deciding How to Act in a Political Society is an exploration into the real world of politics, not from a theoretical stance, but from a participatory and practical one. The book describes the various value conflicts which government representatives face in trying to resolve political issues. The book situates you in various political roles, allowing you to confront your ethical values by comparing them to those operating in the political world. In presenting the various exercises and situations from the point of view of those involved in politics, you will learn that it is difficult, but not impossible, to act politically in a moral manner. In any case, this book rests on the assumption that making political decisions involves "the adjustment of competing claims, managed in the least fractious manner possible. And to this end it enlists the energies of citizens not only as voters, but as joiners in all kinds of civic enterprises" ("Politics as a Spectator Sport," *The New Republic*).

The chapters in this book develop five significant aspects of the political process. The first chapter asks: What is the role of political parties? How effectively do they reflect liberal and conservative positions on various issues? The second chapter focuses on the candidate. What attracts good people to run for office? Are the personal and psychic costs of running too high? The third chapter dramatizes the problems of campaigning. Can a candidate win and still conduct a fair campaign? The fourth chapter examines the problems of officeholders. What can be done to make government more responsive, effective and just? The last chapter looks at the different ways in which citizens can exercise political pressure. Throughout the book you are asked to evaluate where you fit in the political process and what degree of involvement you will choose as citizens.

Here are four situations, typical of other cases in the book. They will give you some feeling for the kinds of problems you will be dealing with. Read each case through. Try to identify what the value conflict is in each case.

Situation 1

While working as a homemaker and raising five children, Pat Pine had served as a volunteer lobbyist for the state association for the mentally retarded. Now, most of her family is grown and Pat is the campaign manager for Mark Daniels, one of the party's promising newcomers. Daniels is giving the incumbent a tough battle for the state senatorial seat. Much of his success is due to Pat's hard work and organizational talents. She dedicates about sixty hours a week to the campaign. One reason that Pat feels such enthusiasm for her candidate is that he is vitally interested in the improvement of health care systems in the state—an issue for which Pat feels personal concern.

Halfway into the campaign, however, the school counselor calls Pat and tells her that her ten-year-old son who is slightly retarded is having problems. If the boy is to continue at the school, he must have more of his mother's attention and help. The counselor advises Pat to discontinue her political activities for the sake of her child. What should Pat do?

Situation 2

The primary election campaign for the attorney general's position is a hotly contested battle between Mike Farrell and Craig Nelson. Both are newcomers to the political scene and both are well-qualified for the job. While soliciting funds from a friend, Mike finds out that Craig was once arrested at a party for possession of marijuana. The charges were later dropped because of insufficient evidence.

Mike feels that this incident has nothing to do with the issues in the campaign. Yet Mike also knows that if the information were made public it could seriously damage his opponent's chances of winning. Craig Nelson has run on a strong law and order platform and counts heavily on his image as a tough prosecutor of crime. How should Mike Farrell deal with this information?

Situation 3

Except for voting in the presidential election every four years, Scott Nielson had never participated in party politics. Then he met Andy Loftus, a youthful, almost charismatic contender for the governor's office. Scott felt that the election of Andy Loftus would not only spell new reforms for his own party but would change the political climate of the state. Already, Loftus had attracted a whole new group of party workers who, like Scott, labored long and hard at precinct caucuses and district conventions to win Loftus's nomination.

At the state convention, the contest for party endorsement involved bitter intra-party struggles. Party regulars tended to support John Meyers, a good man but a middle-of-the-roader, who would offer little challenge to the voter. Older party members saw no need for party reforms, and they tended to regard Loftus, as well as his new party workers, with some suspicion. When the convention reached a stalemate over the endorsement, a third candidate, who had only a small margin of support, threw his delegates to Meyers, thus securing for him the party's endorsement.

Scott was disappointed. He wondered whether he should join with the party regulars in working for Meyers' election or if he should drop out of politics until he finds a candidate he could be committed to.

Situation 4

When Mayor Joseph Strong was elected mayor, he appointed Gail MacGregor, a friend and close political associate, as head of the city's park commission. The city council had appropriated five hundred thousand dollars for a new park, and MacGregor's job was to determine the location. Because of urban redevelopment, a few acres of valuable land is for sale in the core city. Gail would like the park to be situated there since there are no other recreational facilities in the area. Besides this, if the city does not buy the land, it will be sold to real-estate developers who plan to build a twenty floor high-rise apartment building there. This would add to the population density of an already crowded section of the city.

But Mayor Strong wants the park to be located in Lakewood, a residential suburban area. Many of the citizens from that district supported Mayor Strong in his campaign, and they have formed neighborhood coalitions to petition the mayor for a park. Because Mayor Strong does not want to alienate the Lakewood constituents, he tells MacGregor that he wants the park located in Lakewood.

This book will ask you to deal with political dilemmas similar to those above. The cases in this book will call for you to make *political* decisions which include a moral dimension. You will be asked to decide which course of action ought to be taken and to offer good reasons to support your proposals. Each situation is open to a number of "right" solutions. The purpose of the exercises is to help you gain the skills you need for the important and hard work of judging the ethics of political behavior.

Political morality involves more than personal morality. In the latter case, an individual may act in an open, honest and loving way to all the persons he or she comes into contact with. For example, in the first situation described here, Pat Pine would be personally justified in following the counselor's advice if the only consideration was a question of what was right for her and her child. Her problem is that this private decision conflicts with what she feels is her public responsibility.

Making political decisions means deciding questions of morality on a social level. How do you decide between the rights of different individuals and groups when these are in conflict with one another? Sometimes what is good for a group may not be good for a particular individual. For example, if a training rule is established for all on a football team, the coach who allows one player to disregard the rule may be acting unfairly toward the team.

When a person engages in political decision-making, he or she may find their sense of personal morality sorely challenged. Whereas in private life a person can often deal with people and decisions on a one-to-one basis, once inside the political arena, the context changes. "In political life one acts not only as a private person but also as a public person. Additional canons of public morality must be followed. New sets of circumstances and obligations must be taken into account. One acts not only as the private person one is, but also for the community one represents" (Michael Novak, *Choosing Our King*).

Making Prescriptive Judgments

Because questions in our society have become increasingly complex and because the mass media daily saturates us with more information than we can handle, many people are content to make decisions based on instant analyses and snap judgments. They decide something is "right" or "wrong," "good" or "bad" without any effort to evaluate the situation. But unless our judgments are backed by careful analysis of the alternatives of the actions, their various consequences, and the principles involved, the judgments become mere "labels." To label something as "good" or "bad," desirable or undesirable, reinforces our tendency to act on our prejudices rather than upon our reasons. It also "gets us off the hook" from having to act on our convictions.

This book asks that you make judgments of a prescriptive type. Prescriptive judgments set forth what we or others should do. They make a prescription for us, for our group, for our society. "Take two or three pills every three hours for your cold." "Individual freedoms must be preserved at any cost."

Ultimately, prescriptive judgments depend on our ability to back our statements with a value that has some final significance. Something important is at stake! For example, a doctor can argue that his patient must take care of his cold since his survival is involved. A congressperson would argue that the constitution guarantees the individual his freedom and if we neglect any one person's rights, the foundations of our whole government are threatened.

To make a prescriptive judgment, we look at a conflict between the desirability of two or more courses of action which have already been taken or which are proposed. In this conflict we usually have a number of courses of action open—so any judgment means that we have to select among the alternative courses open to us.

As we try to select among the alternatives, however, we really must measure the desirability of the consequences of each alternative. So when we say that in this problem we ought to do "X," "X" is an alternative which we have selected because of our judgment that the probable consequences of that alternative are more desirable (for one reason or another) than the consequences attending the other alternatives.

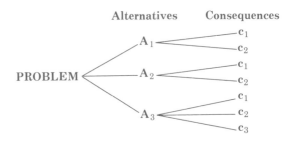

At the point where we judge among consequences, we are dealing with our values. *A value is a specific good that we believe should be fostered.*

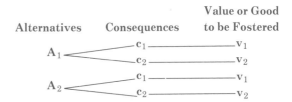

Once we see which values are at stake, we need to decide on some criteria by which certain values ought to be promoted over others. But what reasons can we find to support our choices?

Wanting to know "the reason why" elicits many different kinds of responses. And each response reveals some underlying value. Here is a list of some justifications people make for their choices and the values these reflect.

1) "That's just the way it is! I don't want to say any more about it."

Acceptance of the status quo

2) "_____ (the President, my teacher, my union leader, etc.) always said that this was right and I accept that position."

Reliance upon authority

3) "I've always used Brand X and have become accustomed to it."

Personal convenience

4) "Everyone feels that _____ minority ought to stay in its place and not move into our neighborhood!"

Conformity to majority opinion

5) "If I do that, I'll get better grades."

Self-interest

Although these justifications may be satisfactory to the persons making them, good reasoning depends on our ability to go beyond these kinds of arguments. Prescriptive judgments depend upon our ability to find supportive arguments for our choices, arguments that are grounded in principles reflecting a person's deepest concerns.

For example, one person might argue: All candidates should reveal the sources of their campaign contributions. Such public disclosures are the best way to ensure that campaigns are financed honestly. On the other hand, someone else might argue against public disclosure on the grounds that it violates the individual's right to privacy. Although the persons disagree about the campaign practice, each one justifies his assertion in the light of some higher principle. And these principles reveal the basic life commitments of the persons making the statements.

You will have to decide yourself what constitutes a good argument backing up a value statement. However, simply to decide is not sufficient. People must not only stand for something—they must do something. Moral judgments usually require action. And that action ought to be effective action, doing something positive about the problem at hand.

Handling the Cases

In the following pages, you will face a series of Encounters in which we confront open-ended problems involving questions of political morality. Before you begin to analyze the cases, here are some guidelines which can help you deal with these dilemmas.

1) *Be certain you understand the situation.* Are you in charge of the facts? The person who is best-informed is the person

who eventually can make the wisest judgment. If you don't understand the issue, consult those who do. Take time to learn as much as you can about the issue before moving on.

2) *Check out your feelings*. Do you have some gut-level reaction to a particular case which immediately influences your opinion for or against an issue? For example, you might instinctively feel sympathy for the retarded child in Situation 1. You can test your reactions by asking yourself, what if the campaign manager were the *father* of the child? Or what if the school counselor advised the *candidate* to drop out of a campaign? Would your reactions be different in any of these instances? Sometimes our gut-level feelings get in the way of clear thinking. But often these feelings give us greater insight.

3) *Consider also any information you may have regarding the needs, motives, or intentions of the persons in each situation*. For example, in Situation 2, what if Mike Farrell *intended* to ruin the political career of his opponent by revealing the information about the drug arrest? In Situation 3, what if the party *needed* the help of the youthful new members in order to succeed? Would that affect Scott's decision?

4) *State the conflict in terms of the values at stake*. For example, Pat Pine might describe her conflict as her "duty to family" versus her "responsibility to the community." Mike Farrell might state his value conflict as his opponent's "right to privacy" versus the "public's need to know." Gail MacGregor could explain her conflict as a "duty to obey higher authority" versus her "right to act on principle."

5) *Lay out the alternatives*. Each case proposes at least two alternatives. Be sure to examine what these are. For example, in the case of Scott Nielson, he can choose to: (a) drop out of the party until he finds a candidate he wants to support; (b) remain in the party and work for the party's nominee.

However, besides the alternatives given in each case, use your imagination and understanding to consider as many other alternatives as possible. For example, Scott Nielson could decide to: (c) remain in the party and form a coalition to work for the party reforms he wants; (d) drop out of the party and join an independent party whose aims are closer to his own.

6) *Try to foresee the consequences*. Each alternative involves one or more consequences. To discern what consequences are involved, you must predict or project these

from your understanding of the situation. For example, using the case of Scott Nielson, what are the consequences of the first alternative? If Scott drops out of the party, he will be registering his protest over the election. On the other hand, by dropping out, he may lose his chance to eventually work out any changes in the party. In the second alternative, if Scott remains in the party, his hard work may win him the respect of other workers and he may be able to initiate some of the reforms he wants. You can predict other consequences for the third and fourth alternatives.

7) *Decide on a course of action and justify your choice.* Once you have examined the various choices and their consequences, you can judge what different values are at stake. In order to select one alternative over another, you will need to decide on a value that best justifies your choice. For example, if you think that Scott Nielson should drop out of politics because that is the honest and authentic thing to do, you might appeal to an existentialist principle. People should act authentically regardless of how their action affects others. If you think Mike Farrell should reveal his opponent's secret, you could argue from a utilitarian position, that is, he should act on whatever is good for the greater number.

Step six is the most difficult part of the decision-making process because in it you are forced to think through to those values that you feel most strongly committed to.

Developing Values

While the quality of class discussion is more important than simply reaching a class agreement (a consensus is not always desirable), it is important that you make your own decisions and justify them. The reasoning which you employ is more important in this educational context than getting an answer, or simply repeating what others think is right. Always try to set forth a judgment rather than an opinion—a judgment which is supported by reasons which you can clearly state when questioned and reasons based upon commitments for which you want to stand as a human being. If others disagree with your judgments, demand their reasons and try to figure out all the possible "good reasons" for your position on the problem being discussed.

The final goal of working through these cases is to develop a consistent and responsible set of values—your own values and commitments—which will guide your decisions and actions as citizens. You should also realize that others may decide on a different—and equally valid—set of values.

THE ROLE OF POLITICAL PARTIES

Why Join?

The following situations illustrate some reasons why people choose to subscribe (or not to subscribe) to political parties. Examine each. Compare them with regard to: (1) Whether the choice can be justified politically. (2) How effective each choice might be in influencing public policies. (3) Which choice seems most ethical to you and why.

1) Jan Johnson will not participate in any political party and as a matter of conscience she refuses to vote. In her estimation, politics and politicians are so corrupt that she cannot have anything to do with them.

2) Jack Conway identifies with a particular party because his immigrant grandparents and working-class parents have always subscribed to this party. He values what they value. Jack always votes a straight party ticket without investigating either the particular candidates or the specific issues because "our party has always been the friend of the workingman."

3) Sam Silversmith joins a party in his community which has been run by "party regulars" of a conservative mind-set. Sam wants the party to take a more liberal thrust on issues and his purpose in working for the party is eventually to create reform. In this process, Sam finds that he must compromise his own stand on certain issues in order to get support for some of his proposals.

4) Bill LaChapelle switched his party affiliation last year. The reason is that he received a promotion in the corporation he works for and he is now an executive in the company. At that time his friends and professional associates put pressure on Bill to switch since, they argued, the interests of the company are better served by the party they belong to.

5) Mabel Kolas has joined a "third party" (a party other than one of the two major parties), but not because she believes the party can win in the forthcoming election. Rather, she feels it is important that people have some platform from which to raise those controversial issues that are not debated by either of the major parties: for example, zero population growth, homosexual rights, and public ownership of railways and airlines.

6) Benjamin Lake has decided not to join either of the major parties, but instead will place his money and time at the disposal of a public interest lobbying group. Benjamin

feels that the group's direct pressure on candidates of every party for support of vital legislation increases the "weight" of his vote.

7) Bill Hubling states his political position this way: "Each party—with the right candidate and platform—can buy me for one election." Every election Bill works and votes for the man and his position regardless of the candidate's party affiliation, and he is willing to switch parties whenever he thinks it necessary.

Role of Political Parties

Political parties exist in the United States (and in many other nations) to organize people for programs of action and policy-making. Large masses of citizens can rally around one or another party and support it with their votes, money donations, and, in some cases, volunteer efforts like knocking on prospective voters' doors to seek their votes. Both the Democratic and Republican Parties, for example, have learned that electing a mayor, a state senator, a governor, a congressional representative, or a president requires careful organizational effort: fund-raising; teams of campaign organizers; skillful use of radio and television; effective posters; handbills; and other forms of campaign literature.

Potential officeholders with dynamic ideas for improving city services or reducing unemployment or protecting the environment cannot get *into* the legislative halls or the city council chambers without the kind of organizational strength that a political party can give them. Ralph Nader might get elected to the United States Senate by the Democratic Party in New York, but he would not have much chance in the Empire State if his campaign were being run by the Volunteers for a Better Environment.

Throughout the history of the United

States, the political parties have stood for certain convictions about the government and political action and have attracted people with somewhat similar ideas. For instance, the Federalists of Alexander Hamilton's day emphasized a strong national government as against state power. The Whigs of the 1830's and 1840's stressed a national economic policy: tariff protection, a national bank and a conservative view of public land sales. The Jackson Democrats portrayed themselves as the party of the plain man: they were unalterably opposed to financial speculators and the aristocracy of money. The Republicans, on the other hand, have alternated between a pro-business emphasis and a concern for protection of the individual and human freedom.

Joining a Party

1) People join political parties because they believe parties offer certain advantages. The following statements list some of these. Which, if any, appeal to you? Discuss your reactions with your classmates.

1) You meet people with similar ideas.

2) You have a forum for debating the issues you have a position on.

3) You can help nominate effective candidates.

4) You can clean up "dirty politics."

5) You can have fun working in campaigns.

6) You can fight for your own pocketbook interests.

7) You might want to run for office someday.

8) You can develop your own leadership potential.

9) You can get a better grade in your social studies class.

10) You can get inside information on how government really works.

Are All Parties the Same?

Critics often complain that the two major political parties are not different from each other: they both support whatever is politically popular at the moment, leaving the thoughtful voter with no real choice.

Actually, serious research into the voting records of those in the national congress does not support this criticism. Republicans, by and large, vote "conservatively" while the majority of Democratic legislators support "liberal" proposals in the Congress.

The division of political ideologies into *conservatives* and *liberals* is a useful and illuminating device. These two groups do have basic and important differences in the way they look at the role of government and at the way people are.

The quotations on the following pages will give you some idea as to how these two positions contrast with each other. Read each statement carefully and then try to sum up each position in your own words.

CONSERVATIVE VIEWPOINT	LIBERAL VIEWPOINT

1) *Is human nature perfectible?*

"Human nature suffers irremediably from certain great flaws or faults, which the Christian calls original sin. Men being imperfect, no perfect social order ever can be created" (Russell Kirk).

"A basic assumption of the liberal thinkers (is) that man is endowed with reason and goodness" (Max Lerner). Man is perfectible.

2) *Should we value individual wisdom over the collective judgment of the group?*

The collective experience is superior to the wisdom of the individual. "The individual is foolish but the species is wise" (Edmund Burke).

Liberalism is concerned with "maximizing the individual's freedom to think, to believe, to express and discuss his views." It can be summed up as "the effort to organize liberty socially" (Max Lerner).

3) *Is change essential in a good society?*

The conservative "has an ingrained aversion to changes in his mode of living... his judgments and decisions in the areas of work, play, culture, religion and societal relations are cautious, moderate and predictable" (Clinton Rossiter).

"The word 'liberal' generally describes the party or tendency that promotes change by constitutional means" (Kenneth Minogue).

4) *How important is preserving the present order?*

"Human beings, said Burke, participate in the accumulated experience of their innumerable ancestors ... Ignore this enor-

Succeeding generations actually have more wisdom than earlier ones and by praising "the infant minds of those who lived in

mous bulk of knowledge, or tinker impudently with it, and man is left awfully afloat in a sea of emotions and ambitions" (Russell Kirk).

an earlier age," we reverse the honored adage and say: "The mother of wisdom is inexperience" (Jeremy Bentham).

5) *How much progress should a good society promote?*

Conservatives "prefer the devil they know to the devil they do not know. Order and justice and freedom are the artificial products of many centuries of trial and error and reflection" (Russell Kirk).

Liberals believe that the enemy of human progress is "custom, tradition, institutions, social habit." They seek "to lift from men what Jefferson called the 'dead hand of the past'" (Max Lerner).

6) *Should society reward some persons because of their "natural superiority"?*

Conservatives believe "some men *are* superior and it is both fair and socially benevolent to reward their superior qualities by high income, marks of deference, or both" (Reo Christenson).

"Liberty without equality is a name of noble sound and squalid meaning" (L.T. Hobhouse).

7) *How can we best utilize government to solve our problems?*

"An American political conservative, at least in popular usage, is a person who believes strongly that the old pattern of American society ought not be much altered ...(He) endeavors to oppose the tendency toward political centralization... and looks uneasily upon the increase of taxation and the 'welfare' roles of the state" (Russell Kirk).

"Liberalism encompasses strong tendencies hostile to anything more than a minimum amount of state regulation of social life and, on the other hand, equally strong tendencies to employ the state's power of compulsion to solve a variety of problems ranging from racial prejudice to industrial pollution" (Kenneth Minogue).

Political parties take generally either a liberal or conservative stance. In other words, their main body of supporters subscribe to one view or the other of the nation's affairs. Liberal parties, of course, may have conservative blocs, for example, the Southern conservatives in the Democratic Party. Conservative parties may have liberal factions, also, such as the Ripon Society and its Republican spokesmen in the Congress.

Examine the following political opinions:
a) Circle the numbers of the statements you favor.

b) Identify each statement as "conservative" or "liberal" and give the reason for your judgment. (For some of the opinions, both answers may be correct depending on the reasons given).

c) On the basis of your answers to a and b, do you identify more with the conservative or liberal thrust?

1) _____ The government should not give anyone financial assistance that he or she has not earned.

2) _____ History teaches us that a strong defense policy is essential to our national security.

3) _____ Our legislatures should pass laws to provide scholarships for any young persons whose potential is blocked by lack of money.

4) _____ The government that governs best governs least.

5) _____ Large scale corporation farming in the United States is a serious threat to all rural private enterprise.

6) _____ We should adopt a national health insurance plan run by the federal government rather than one operated by the private insurance companies.

7) _____ The careless spending and high tax policies of state governments should be reversed.

8) _____ Everyone has the right to bear arms and therefore the government has no business registering guns.

9) _____ We oppose full-time legislators since people are better represented by those who make their living working among their constituents.

10) _____ We urge a fundamental revision of sex roles in our society to permit both men and women full expression of themselves in all areas of life.

11) _____ The present system of jails and prisons is unworkable and has a hundred year history of failure.

12) _____ The penalties for selling marijuana to minors should be increased and existing laws enforced.

The Two Party System

Political scientist Reo Christenson of Miami University of Ohio describes the need for both conservatives and liberals in this striking passage from *Heresies, Right and Left:* "Every nation needs intelligent liberals and intelligent conservatives. Emerson wrote, 'Each is a great half but an impossible whole. Each exposes the abuses of the other but in a true society, in a true man, both must combine.' We need liberals to criticize and to offer corrective proposals; we need conservatives to ask the hard searching questions that force liberals to prove they have done their homework and have thought things through."

There are no "pure" liberals or conservatives. Some candidates are "liberal" on some issues and "conservative" on others. Observers have remarked that the differences between parties in American politics are not always so distinctive as the differences that often crop up within the *one* party that happens to be in power.

Tweedledum and Tweedledee

Consider a national campaign where both major parties appear to offer "no choice" to the voter because both candidates say much the same thing. Such was the opinion of many voters about the 1968 contest between Hubert Humphrey and Richard Nixon. One British journalist dubbed the antagonists as Tweedledum and Tweedledee. Both men promised to end the Vietnam War quickly and to fight inflation with very similar programs. Because many voters could see little difference in their positions, large numbers of Americans stayed away from the polls. The result was a very narrow margin of victory for Nixon.

1) Find a newspaper account of the 1968 Presidential race written right after the election, and read it.

2) In the attempt to get elected, do candidates necessarily have to "play down" differences so as to appeal to the widest number of people?

3) Do you think that there was a real choice in 1968? (Consult Theodore H. White's *The Making of the President 1968* or *The American Melodrama* by L. Chester, G. Hodgson and B. Page.)

4) If you believed there was no real choice, how would you decide? By party preference? Would you refuse to vote?

A Matter of Clear Defeat

In 1964 and 1972 voters were offered "clear choice" candidates: Republican Barry Gold-

water and Democrat George McGovern.

Goldwater offered the nation, as Theodore H. White pointed out, "a whole series of choices, a whole system of ideas which clashed with the governing ideas that had ruled America for a generation." Goldwater proposed a tougher defense posture against Communism, a voluntary system of social security, and a substantial decrease in the strength of the central government.

McGovern, like Goldwater before him, believed "that the American government was the enemy of the American people" (Theodore H. White). He advocated a 37 percent reduction in the defense budget with the savings going to social welfare. He proposed far-reaching tax reforms that would plug all loopholes and promised one thousand dollars to every person in America.

Both men were rejected by the voters with the two most lopsided defeats in the history of American presidential elections.

1) Would you conclude that American voters are hesitant to support candidates offering real change? If not, why not?

2) Do you think either Goldwater or McGovern should have modified or altered his positions in order to win the election?

3) If you were running for president, would you change one of your positions because it was unpopular with the voters?

The Pressure of Third Parties

When the voters feel that neither major party is addressing itself effectively to issues they believe are vitally important—for example, law and order, tax reform, excessive presidential power, rising inflation and rising unemployment—the appeal of a third-party force often becomes very strong. Vigorous leaders with bold programs may emerge to capture the imaginations of the discontented.

On the presidential level of American campaign politics, third parties have been influential at certain times. The Populists in 1896, the Bull Moose Party in 1912, the Dixiecrats in 1948—for example—all drew either a sizable number of popular votes or a significant number of electoral votes away from the Democratic and Republican parties.

In 1968, George Wallace ran against Nixon and Humphrey as the candidate of the American Party. Wallace had so much strength in Alabama, Georgia, Louisiana, Mississippi, and Arkansas that many respected observers thought he would get a large enough bloc of electoral votes to prevent either of the national parties from getting a majority. A month before the election, the *New York Times* declared that Wallace was running ahead of Humphrey.

Wallace wound up with 47 electoral votes

and five states in his column on election day. But before the election, Wallace was rated by both rival camps as a threat. In fact, Wallace appeared on national television and talked of winning because one of the other candidates, he claimed, would throw his votes to Wallace in the electoral college.

1) Do you see any indication of a third party movement in the next presidential election? Explain.

2) What issues in your opinion would be important enough to cause a third party to form? What other issues do you think a third party would have to adopt to gain a broad enough base?

This fictional story describes a three party split in a school election.

"Three's a Crowd"

Mary Brovelli is the first girl candidate for president of the student council in the history of Central High. She is running mainly on the issue of student participation in decision-making. She pledges that, if elected, she will encourage student council members to seek student consensus on important issues.

Her opponent is Thor Nelson, football captain and advocate of a "tight ship" style of running the council. "We'll make the decisions," he says, "because we'll have more facts than the student body."

Many of the students are disaffected with the undemocratic way in which student government was run in the past and they lean favorably towards Mary. However, a third candidate is running: Joe Hill, editor of an underground paper at Central called "The Subterranean Echo." Joe promises, if elected, to fight for a student-run newspaper free of censorship and faculty control.

1) If only two candidates were running, Mary and Thor, how do you think the election would go?

2) Does Joe Hill's running cut into Mary's vote or into Thor's vote? Explain.

3) Consider and discuss how Joe Hill should react to offers of a "coalition," a partnership in the election. For example, Mary might ask Joe to support her bid. His support would ensure her victory in the election, she says, and she then could work for many of the school reforms they both feel are important, including a censorship-free newspaper. What do you think Joe would reply?

How would Joe react if Thor asks him for his help in order to save the student council from control by a woman?

4) In your opinion, could Joe Hill win a three-way race? Why or why not?

5) What conclusion would you draw from this case about the role of third parties and their influence on the major parties?

The Parties' Effect on Government

Although our political process traditionally works through a two-party system, once either of the major parties gains a plurality of votes, that party becomes a central force in determining public policy. For example, the dominant party forms a voting bloc within the legislature exercising control over the passage or non-passage of bills. The members of the majority party also control appointments to government jobs.

The following two fictional cases give you an idea of how party affiliation affects political choices.

A Political Dilemma

As a dedicated member of the Democratic Party in a large city, you would normally support all Democratic candidates for office in the area. This year the party has endorsed Joe Doyle for city council. You have known Joe for a long time, and both of you have worked long and hard for the party. However, you personally believe that Joe is not qualified to serve as a city councilman. You worked against his endorsement for the job but failed to convince the leaders of the local party. Your primary objection to Joe is that he is simply not bright enough or quick enough to handle the job.

The Republicans, on the other hand, have endorsed an intelligent young attorney, Sven Fjord, whom you very much respect. Although you are a loyal Democrat, you feel that Sven would be a more productive member of the city council. With this in mind, you stay out of the campaign.

Toward the end of the race, however, the county chairman of your party approaches you and indicates that the battle for control of the city council is so close that it hangs on the outcome of the Doyle campaign.

The chairman pleads with you to get involved, saying that Democratic effectiveness in the council depends on this race.

1) In trying to decide what to do, what are the advantages that you must consider and what are the disadvantages of supporting Doyle's candidacy? What would be the consequences of each choice?

2) In your opinion, is party loyalty more important in this case than the relative abilities of the candidates? Justify your answer.

The Party in Power

You have recently been elected to the state legislature from Greenwood, a growing suburban area. As a Republican running in what was once a predominantly Democratic area, you are generally viewed as an up-and-coming leader in your party. The press views your victory as a major upset in this year's election and you have received countless letters and telegrams of congratulations from all levels of political leadership.

You have spent the interim between the election and your being sworn into office developing an elaborate program of environmental protection for the state. This is your special area of interest and also that of many of your constituents.

Upon arriving in the capitol on the first day of the new session, you must face these critical problems. First, the majority party always elects the house speaker and therefore, in this session, the house speaker will be a Democrat. Secondly, the speaker controls all committee appointments and also schedules when bills will be debated on the floor. Thirdly, the legislature runs on a seniority system. As only one of three freshmen legislators, you are at the bottom of the totem pole as far as influence is concerned.

Although you had requested to be put on the Environmental Protection Committee, the speaker appoints you to the Agriculture Committee. He explains that by the time he got to you in the selection process, all the seats on the Environmental Committee had been filled. You feel frustrated and you wonder how you are going to fulfill the pledges you made to your constituents concerning new legislation to protect the environment.

1) In the legislative process, how does the influence of the individual legislator compare with that of the political party in power?

2) If you were a voter from Greenwood who was interested in getting environmental protection legislation passed, what means would be available to you? What do you think would be the most effective way of reaching your goal?

The next two cases, one actual and one fictional, illustrate how seniority and legislative experience favor an incumbent.

The Senior Senator

In the summer of 1974, one of the major primary contests for the United States Senate was in the state of Arkansas. The two major candidates were Senator William Fulbright, a five-term senator, and Governor Dale Bumpers, who had no elected experience at the national level.

Senator Fulbright had emerged on the national scene as a major figure in foreign affairs. He ultimately became the chairman of the Senate Foreign Affairs Committee and an influential voice in controlling the direction that foreign policy was taking in this country. As a five-term senator, he obviously had a great deal of seniority in the congress.

Governor Bumpers had just finished his first term as governor of Arkansas and was extremely popular with the people of the state. It was this popularity among other things that led Bumpers to challenge the veteran senator.

The campaign focused on the issue of seniority in Congress versus closer contact with the voters back in Arkansas. Fulbright campaigned on the issue that with his experience and seniority in the Senate, along with his international reputation in foreign affairs, he could do more for the citizens of Arkansas by trade-offs, soliciting liberal senators' support for legislation affecting local Arkansas interests.

Bumpers contended that Fulbright was too busy as committee chairman to take care of the daily concerns of the people of Arkansas. He argued that it was better for the people of Arkansas to have a senator who spent more time on local problems.

1) Who would you have voted for had you lived in Arkansas in 1974? Why?

2) Which do you think was Senator Fulbright's greater responsibility—chairing the Senate Foreign Relations Committee or working for the local interests of his constituents back in Arkansas? Explain the reasons for your answer.

The Incumbent's Influence

Representative Arnold Johnson is your state representative. He has represented your district for the past ten years and is the House Majority Leader. As such, he is a powerful figure in state government.

The district you live in is in the southern part of the state. Unemployment is a serious problem, and the major industries are logging, tourism, and paper mills.

The district is heavily Republican. Johnson has not had a Democratic opponent for the past six years. But this year Bob Crowell, a Republican, is opposing Johnson in the Republican primary.

The major issue is a new national park. Crowell is opposed to the park and many people agree with him. The park, Crowell argues, will mean a decrease in the number of jobs available in the paper and logging industry. And this, he says, coupled with a large number of environmental actions taken by the state legislature during the past session, will make the entire district into nothing but a playground for tourists.

Johnson, who as House Majority Leader did not oppose much of the environmental legislation, argues that, in the long run, the district will benefit financially from the park and the legislation.

In any event, he says the legislation has already passed; the park will be built and nothing he or Crowell can do or say will stop it. "Our only alternative," he says, "is to make sure we don't lose jobs in the process."

Johnson points out that Crowell, if elected, would be a freshman legislator and powerless to help the district.

"As majority leader," he says, "I can do something about the problem of jobs."

As a voter, you feel that the district would benefit from much of the environmental legislation. You support the park. On the other hand, Johnson seems to make sense when he says that as majority leader he can do more than Crowell to provide new jobs.

1) What is the value conflict in this case?

2) What might be the consequences of voting for either candidate?

This fictional case asks you to deal with the constant tension an officeholder may feel between his or her political philosophies and membership in a party.

Party Pressure

As a member of the state legislature, you are faced with a difficult vote in the last hours of your first session. You are a member of the majority party in the legislature but the margin of the majority is two votes. The governor, who is also a member of your party, has proposed a sales tax increase of one cent across the board. You personally are opposed to the sales tax concept and in your last campaign said that you would not support a sales tax increase. Several other members of your party in the legislature made the same commitment. If all the members who oppose the sales tax concept vote against it, the governor's entire tax package will be defeated.

The speaker of the house calls you into his office, along with other members who oppose the sales tax. He tries to convince you to support the governor's tax program. He points out that the governor would be embarrassed if members of his own party did not support him on the tax program. He also points out that most of the money raised by the increase in sales tax will go for senior citizen property tax relief.

1) What values are in conflict here?

2) What would be the consequences of each choice?

3) How would you vote: pro, con, or abstain. Explain your decision.

Intra-Party Conflicts

"I don't belong to an organized political party, I'm a Democrat."

Will Rogers

Long-lasting and often bitter feuds develop between the various wings and factions within each major party. These factions compete with each other for power in local, state, and national conventions, at party caucuses, and in primary elections. Once the issues are settled or the candidate is selected, parties traditionally unite and come together. In some instances, however, the opposing factions never do reconcile their differences. The result is usually a lost election.

Most polls show Democrats outnumber Republicans by almost two to one. In theory, Democrats should never lose a national election, but in fact, they did lose in 1968 and in 1972, largely because of splits in their party. Consider the following two cases about conflicts within the Democratic Party.

"Bossism" in Chicago?

In 1968, Senator Eugene McCarthy, at the forefront of the anti-war movement, was challenging the party regulars' choice of Hubert Humphrey for the Democratic presidential nomination.

Humphrey had the majority of delegates to the national convention and was thus assured of the nomination, but McCarthy's supporters were challenging the delegate selection process. They felt cheated and charged that the selection process deliberately excluded women and other minorities. They thought the system was "rigged" in favor of the party regulars whom they charged with "bossism." The violence that erupted in Chicago that year triggered a deep and serious split in the Democratic Party.

Many political analysts attributed Humphrey's subsequent defeat to the Chicago convention. Many of McCarthy's supporters dropped out of politics, disillusioned and cynical; others remained but refused to support Humphrey.

1) Do you think that supporters of a defeated candidate (e.g., McCarthy) should support the candidate of the entire party? Why or why not?

2) Can you determine from newspaper articles of that election what were the consequences of the loss of McCarthy supporters from the 1968 campaign? Do you think that the consequences were eventually justified or not?

The "Bosses" Lose

Party leaders, in an attempt to unite the

party after the 1968 election, appointed a reform commission to study the delegate selection process. Senator George McGovern was selected to chair the commission.

The McGovern Commission presented a series of "affirmative action" proposals to guide the delegate selection process. The new system required that certain numbers of women and other minorities be selected as delegates.

The McGovern Commission proposals, adopted in 1971, were bitterly opposed by many of the party regulars. They saw the proposals as an attempt by the New Left to usurp their power.

As the 1972 election approached, it became clear that the reform proposals would have a dramatic effect on the Democratic National Convention. Taking full advantage of his commission's proposals, George McGovern easily won his party's nomination. Many of those who were in the Chicago streets in 1968 found themselves serving as delegates in 1972. And many of the 1968 power brokers found themselves watching the 1972 convention on television.

Mayor Richard Daley of Chicago, who in 1968 had practically handpicked the entire Illinois delegation, was successfully challenged and removed from the 1972 convention for failure to comply with the McGovern guidelines.

George Meany, the head of the powerful AFL-CIO—the largest labor organization in the country—was outraged at the reforms and became openly hostile to McGovern. For the first time, the AFL-CIO did not support the Democratic nominee for President.

Just as the party "reformers" sat out the 1968 election, many of the party "regulars" sat out 1972. And while it's far too simple to say that the party reforms were responsible for the defeat of McGovern in 1972, they were certainly a contributing factor.

1) Do you think the behavior of the Democratic regulars in 1972 was different from that of the McCarthy supporters in 1968? Why or why not?

2) Was there any way in 1972 for the Democrats to achieve reform and still maintain party unity? Discuss.

Besides the questions of reform within a party, there is also the problem of factions that threaten party solidarity. Consider the following fictional case.

A Dangerous Split

As a delegate to your state party convention, you are strongly supporting Benjamin

Grant, a black legislator, for Governor. There are a number of issues you are interested in but you feel most strongly about gun control, campaign reform, and improved health care.

Grant has taken a strong stand in favor of restricting the sale of handguns, has been a leader in the fight for campaign reform, and has proposed an impressive series of health care measures.

His opponent for the gubernatorial nomination is Senator J. Williams Lowell. Lowell considers himself a moderate and while he has said that he is in favor of campaign reform, he hasn't been very specific. You've spoken to him several times regarding health care proposals but he just doesn't seem very interested. When asked about gun control, Senator Lowell said he'd have to study the matter before he made up his mind.

The incumbent governor, a conservative of the other party, has easily won his party's nomination for another term and will be extremely tough to beat in November. During his current term of office, he vetoed three campaign reform bills, has repeatedly said he's opposed to any form of gun control, and appointed four of his political cronies to the State Health Board.

The rules under which your convention operates provide that a candidate for governor must win 60 percent of the delegates' vote to get the party's endorsement. Both candidates have said they would not run in a primary against an endorsed candidate.

However, the convention has voted fifteen times and neither Lowell nor Grant has gotten the required 60 percent. There are six hundred delegates and that means that three hundred and sixty-one votes are needed. On the last ballot, Lowell received 354 votes or just 7 short of endorsement.

Shortly after the last ballot was announced, you are approached by Jane Klein, your legislative district leader and a strong supporter of Lowell. Jane asks you to switch your vote from Grant to Lowell. The vote is so close that your vote plus a few others will make the difference. She reminds you that the convention will adjourn shortly and if neither candidate gets the endorsement, a primary election will be necessary. She points out that a primary might split the party, and that it would cost a great deal of money that could be better spent defeating the incumbent in November. You agree that Lowell would make a better governor than the incumbent, but you are still convinced that Grant is the better candidate.

1) What values are in conflict?
2) Could you be flexible enough in this case to vote for Lowell, your second choice? Explain your reasons.

SENSITIVITY MODULES:
Discovering and Expressing

1) Clip the editorials from five different newspapers. Examine them to determine whether the editor's philosophy is more liberal or conservative.

2) Have the class call a candidate in your area who is seeking endorsement from one of the major parties. Have the candidate come to your class and explain why he or she deserves the endorsement. Try to find a candidate in your area who is running without party endorsement. Ask that person also why he or she does not feel that endorsement is necessary.

3) Select any bill that is up for passage in your state legislature and follow its progress through the committees on to the floor. Attend open sessions to see how both sides are represented on the issue.

4) Conduct a poll among your neighbors to find out how many of the people you interview are registered as Democrats or Republicans. How many people said that they were Independents, voters who do not declare for a particular party? Ask each of the people you talk to, to give their reasons for belonging or not belonging to a particular party.

5) Write to the local party headquarters of the major parties and ask for copies of the platforms from their state conventions. Have different members of the class compare and contrast the introductions and sections on certain key issues.

Suggested Readings

Buckley, William F. *Up from Liberalism.* New York: Macdowell, Obolensky, 1959. A witty analysis by one of America's leading political conservatives.

Christenson, Reo M. *Heresies Right and Left: Some Political Assumptions Re-examined.* Paperback ed. New York: Harper & Row, 1973.

McCarthy, Eugene. *The Limits of Power.* Paperback ed. New York: Dell, 1968.

National Review. A leading magazine of conservative political opinion.

New Republic. A leading magazine of liberal political opinion.

Novak, Michael. *Choosing Our King.* New York: Macmillan, 1974. A stimulating discussion of political morality and political symbols, especially Parts Two, Four and Five.

Rossiter, Clinton, *Parties and Politics in America.* Paperback ed. New York: Mentor Books, 1960. Difficult but very solid source.

THE CANDIDATE

Politicians Are . . .

The following list contains some words which many people use to describe politicians. Circle any of the terms which seem to express your feelings about most politicians.

1) crooked
2) egotistical
3) honest
4) unethical
5) responsible
6) moral
7) shady
8) courageous
9) forthright
10) hypocritical

If you're like many people, you circled the more uncomplimentary terms in the exercise above. Examine your reasons for choosing the terms you did. Do you know any politicians personally? Do any of the terms you checked apply to them? Are you judging politicians mainly on what you hear on the radio, see on television, or read in the newspapers?

In the United States, we have regarded politicians with suspicion since the days that the colonists fought with Britain over unjust tax laws. Other nations have similar traditions of distrust.

Explain the following statements and tell why you agree or disagree with each one.

1) "I am not a politician and my other habits are good" (Artemus Ward).

2) "A statesman is a politician who has been dead for ten or fifteen years" (Harry S. Truman).

3) "It is doubtful whether man is enough of a political animal to produce a good, sensible, serious, and efficient constitution. All evidence is against it" (George Bernard Shaw).

4) "Practical politics consists in ignoring facts" (Henry Adams).

5) "What would be your advice to young people considering entering into politics?" "I would advise them to stay out of it" (Gordon Strachan in the Watergate Hearings).

The Need for Politics and Political Leaders

Although it may be the fashion for some Americans to ridicule politics and downgrade politicians, the American system rests on the conviction that politics is absolutely necessary—the only way to ensure that democratic rule continues in the United States.

Bernard Crick, a distinguished British political scientist, has pointed out that many people in the modern world "think that politics is muddled, contradictory, unimpressive, unpatriotic, inefficient, mere compromise, or even a sham or conspiracy . . ." But from the time of Aristotle's *Politics* to the present day, serious political thinkers have pointed out that politics is the only way to prevent competing groups and interests from tearing a nation apart. Politics is the civilized man's answer to the threat of tyranny or dictatorship.

Why is this so? Because politics is an art of conciliation, an intelligent working out of the conflicts that arise when a great number of differing groups (as in a nation like the United States) push their own traditions, points of view, and public goals.

Politics in a democracy gives every group a fair hearing in an orderly way. It rejects the bullying tactics of "the strong man"

leader and the fanatical excesses of political parties or pressure groups who think that "only they know best" what is right for all the people of a nation. Democratic politics encourages open competition among all groups; it allows for reasonable compromise and practical solutions for the extremely complex problems that often face a country.

Politicians are women or men who understand the essential need for politics and who practice this art. In a democratic society, politicians should be able to resist quick answers, the resort to force, the stifling of open debate or free speech. They should know that they will succeed only by being willing to listen to others and by studying carefully the complexities involved in political decisions.

Politicians should know by experience and from history that politics keeps a country from the violence and chaos that accompany all efforts to rule a nation without politics.

Who Should Run for Office?

A candidate for public office is ideally a person who aspires to political leadership. To evaluate how effective a candidate will be if elected, the voter has to understand what political leadership requires: for example, the ability to listen and to compromise; the ability to understand people and work with various groups.

You Make the Choice

Electing student body officers in a high school is similar to electing public officials. The following candidates are running for student body president of Eisenhower High. How would you evaluate the "political" potential of each?

Fred Janascek: Fred is co-captain of the undefeated Eisenhower football team. He is president of the Letterman's Club and extremely popular with the student body. It is evident that the faculty respects him because of his aggressive performance on the field as defensive captain. A steady worker in school, Fred's campaign slogan is "Janascek Will Unite Us."

Karen Barrett: Karen is a National Merit semi-finalist and for the last three years has earned a straight "A" average. The faculty respects her for her intellectual ability, and she is president of the school's Latin Club. Karen is rather aloof and socializes mainly with those students who, like herself, are strong in academic areas. However, she expresses herself well and attacks problems with energy. She is big on "student rights" and recently wrote an article on "Student Freedom" for the local morning daily.

Martha Kaplan: Martha is a quiet and reserved person. She chums around with a small group of girls who do volunteer work at the local hospital. Martha is the kind of person people count on to do the hard, "behind-the-scenes" work like painting the props for the class play. Everyone is surprised she is running because she is basically a shy person, but Martha has definite ideas on giving women students a more active role in student government. She is also working for student involvement in such community projects as tutoring poor children and helping the elderly care for their homes.

Debby Walker: The daughter of a prominent local judge, Debby is something of a glamor girl at Eisenhower: pretty, personable, and out-going. Debby's family has been active in city politics for two generations, and Debby has a knack for clever campaign posters and other vote-getting techniques. She has been successful in promoting better attendance at football and basketball games, and getting top local rock groups for school dances.

Joe Sanchez: Joe is very sharp, articulate and shrewd. He is the star of the debate team and instinctively fights against what he feels are violations of student rights. He took on the administration during his junior year over the issue of the conservative dress code. He's ready to fight the administration again this year on such issues as teacher evaluation and the freedom of the student newspaper to editorialize as it wishes.

1) In a primary, which of the five would you vote for and why?

2) What standards did you use for evaluating the candidates? Why? How difficult was the choice?

3) If this were your school, which two candidates would emerge from the primary to run in the final election? Explain the reasons for your opinion.

Why Do People Run for Public Office?

People reach the decision to run for office in a number of ways. Some come to the decision to run for office as a natural conclusion to their personal interest in politics or government in general. Others become involved through their interest in a specific issue or area; they see the political process as a means of influencing or winning that issue.

Perhaps the vast majority of people become candidates not through a deliberate effort on their part but through pressure from friends and associates who decide that the person would be a good choice to serve in a particular office. There are, of course, other factors involved. Motives play an important role. An individual's character, personality, educational background—in short, his or her personal environment—all contribute to the degree of motivation necessary for deciding to become a candidate.

Consider how you might act if you found yourself in the following situation.

The School Board Dilemma

You are a recent college graduate, employed by the Peerless Insurance Agency. You are very familiar with your town's educational system, and while you know there are some problem areas, you are favorably impressed with the system as a whole. At a Chamber of Commerce meeting one day, you discover there is a vocal element present that feels strongly that the school system needs a radical overhaul. You hear them complaining about the lack of discipline in the school, the "dirty books" in the library, the easy-going teachers, and the basketball team's losing record.

Bradley Bradshaw, the Chamber's secretary/treasurer, announces a week later that he is running for the school board to voice the complaints of the Chamber's school critics.

You resent the criticism you've heard and particularly the negative attitude of the people it's coming from. You know there are many people who feel as you do, but you're not sure they're willing to oppose the negative critics. You think Bradshaw has a good chance of winning, and it appears that many Chamber members are supporting him.

A week goes by and it appears that nobody in the community is going to run against Bradshaw. You think this is an unfortunate situation, and while discussing it with a close friend, he suggests that you run for the vacant seat.

You think about it overnight, and intrigued with the idea, you discuss it with your boss. He points out to you that many of the Chamber members who are supporting Bradshaw are also good clients of the Peerless Agency. He says it may not be good business to alienate them and wants to know how much time away from Peerless the campaign and school board job will take. He does agree that Bradshaw would be a poor choice for the board, but he leaves the final decision to you.

That evening, the president of your local PTA calls and asks you to run.

1) What do you tell her and why? Before making your decision, what questions would you ask yourself?

2) What are the rewards in an office such as this? What is the price? Is it worth it?

3) Is this a decision you must make for yourself or can other people make it for you? Who should be consulted?

4) What if you don't think you can win? Should you run anyway? Why or why not?

Political analysts observe that people run for office for other reasons than public service. Here are some reasons why people say they run for political office. Which of these would appeal to you and why?

1) "Politics is exciting: the rallies, the TV ads, the handshaking. Once you've caught the bug, you can't stay out of the arena."

2) "I like politics because it gives me a feeling of power—the opportunity to help shape the lives and futures of people around me."

3) "Everyone wants to be popular. I like limousines, banquets, public applause; and especially, the respect politics brings."

4) "I'd like my name in the history books, so that future generations will know I did something worthwhile with my life."

5) "You won't get rich in politics, but you will get connections with those who are wealthy. And that will pay off, one way or the other."

The Personal Costs of Running

"My wife and my family have paid a very high price for my political career, and I regret that. I've had to travel through the district and over the country. I've been out many, many evenings and weekends. I've missed birthdays, anniversaries, confirmations, school plays. I've neglected my children and forced my wife to neglect them, because I need to have her with me at political functions. In politics you cannot have a normal family life. Politics is carried over into whatever you are doing. It affects all your actions and thoughts, and those of your wife and children. You live in a goldfish bowl. . . . Your moods, your thoughts, your entire conversation are determined by politics."

Robert A. Liston

The consensus of practicing politicians is that no other profession places more strain on a person and his or her family than the pressure-cooker politics prevalent in the United States. Does the American political system discourage potentially good candidates from running for office? Let us examine some of the specific problems that often produce "drop-outs" from the world of politics.

The Crowded Calendar

A politician's time is not his or her own. The voting public demands from its elected officials a strict accounting of time. Besides his official duties, the politician must harken to the requests of community groups, of schools and universities to speak at their functions and meetings. And then there are the ceremonial duties of office: parades, banquets, award ceremonies.

The officeholder must also maintain vital contact with other units of government in order to remain abreast of developing issues and complexities. In addition, there are numerous phone calls, letters and personal conferences which must be attended to.

Time Out

Sam Johnson is a teacher in a senior high social studies department, and he is chairman of the local ward club. Sam has been asked by a number of close friends and political allies to run for the state legislature.

Sam knows from personal experience that campaigning takes time—lots of time. He wonders how he should reconcile his responsibilities to his job and to his family with the need to run an all-out campaign. As a teacher, Sam has an advantageous working schedule. His last class ends at 3:30 p.m. and he can easily be home by 4:00 o'clock. The administration has indicated they will allow him time off to campaign for the office since the campaign exposure will bring good publicity to the school.

Sam's wife Lois is not very enthusiastic about her prospective new role as a representative's wife. She worries about what may happen to the family during the hard months of campaigning and after. She works full-time to supplement the family income.

Sam's three children are all under ten years of age. Two of the children are beginning scouting activities in the evening and require transportation to and from the meeting. The third child, the oldest, is a football player and practices five nights a week. His games are on Saturday morning.

On the following page is the appointment calendar which the campaign committee has submitted to Sam. Read it carefully and then answer the following questions:

1) Look at the calendar for Friday, October 8. On that day, Sam's son will be graduated from the Cub scouts to the Weblos. How would you resolve the time conflicts if you were in Sam's place?

2) Wednesday, October 27, is Lois' birthday. What problems face Sam? How do you think he should resolve them?

October

SUNDAY	MONDAY	TUESDAY	WEDNESDAY	THURSDAY	FRIDAY	SATURDAY
					1 6:00-factory gate U.A.W. 4:00-door knocking 8:00-Town & Country banquet	**2** 9:00-literature drop 2:00-campaign meeting
3 1:00-door knocking	**4** 10:00-Hearing-for metro & urban affairs 4:00-door knocking	**5** 6:00-factory gate Westinghouse Plant 12:00-speech-for citizens forum 8:00-U.A.W. mtg.	**6** 6:00-factory gate (Ford Motor Co.) 3:00-door knocking 7:30-citizens forum meeting	**7** 10:00-comm. mtg. 3:30-door knocking 6:00-League W. Voters	**8** 6:00-Westinghouse gate 2:30-public hearing P.C.A. 4:00-door knocking	**9** 9:00-literature drop 2:00-campaign meeting 8:00-fundraiser—my house
10 1:00-door knocking 3:00-mtg.	**11** 6:00-Auto Workers breakfast speech 12:00-Lunch—Highway's-Gedar Bridge 4:00-door knocking	**12** 11:30-Rotary speech 3:00-door knocking 8:00-N.S.P. Council	**13** 6:00-Factory gate—Ford Plant 9:00-St. Paul 3:00-door knocking 7:30-P.T.A.—Candidates mtg.	**14** 10:00-Johnson H.S. 12:00-speech A.L. 4:00-door knocking 8:00-V.F.W.	**15** 12:00-Luncheon 7:00-fundraiser	**16** 1:00-door knocking 2:00-literature drop 7:30-J.C. Banquet
17 1:00-door knocking	**18** 6:00-factory U.A.W. 12:00-Staff lunch 3:00-door knocking 8:00-Metro League mtg.	**19** 6:00-U.A.W. gate 12:00-Lunch K.V. 1:00-staff 4:00-door knocking	**20** 7:00-Citizens League 10:00-B.T.'s lunch 5:00-mtg.	**21** 10:00-comm. mtg. 12:00-Rotary luncheon 4:00-door knocking 7:00-cand. mtg.	**22** 6:00-factory gate (Westinghse.) 12:00-C. of C. speech 4:00-door knocking 8:00-Union mtg.-Trades Assembly	**23** 9:00-seminar Democratic campaign procedures 1:00-door knocking
24 1:00-door knocking 3:00-phone bank	**25** 7:30-Breakfast mtg. 4:00-door knocking	**26** 4:00-door knocking 8:00-City Council Maplewood	**27** Wife's birthday 1:00-door knocking 2:30-campaign mtg. 4:00-door knocking 8:00-PTA speech	**28** 7:15-Shoreview Candidates mtg.	**29** 8:00-fundraiser VFW Hall	**30** 3:00-staff

3) Sam gave his American Government class a big test on Wednesday, October 13. Grades are due on Friday, the 15. What conflicts does this cause for Sam? How would you resolve the problem?

4) On Tuesday, June 19, it is raining heavily. Two of Sam's campaign workers call to ask if he still plans to go door-knocking. Sam himself is not feeling up to par. How would you answer if you were in his place?

The Loss of Privacy

Politicians live their lives in the glare of publicity. The people demand from their officeholders a "public image" or "face." To look foolish, to be less than sure, to admit mistakes, is inconsistent with the image the public wants and a sure ticket to defeat at the polls. Literally, every action a politician takes must be considered within the public and political context of possible consequences.

The loss of privacy coupled with the necessity for always appearing alert, in command, may seem to smack of a superman mentality, but it is what the public often demands. An incident in the 1972 presidential primaries illustrates the problem.

Muskie at Manchester

At the start of the 1972 presidential campaign, Senator Edmund Muskie was the leading contender for the Democratic nomination. Muskie projected a Lincolnesque image: a tall, cool, imperturbable Yankee. While Muskie was campaigning in New Hampshire, the editor of the *Manchester Union Leader,* Edward Loeb, published a defamatory story accusing Muskie of using ethnic slurs and picturing Muskie's wife as a vulgar woman.

With brusque determination, Muskie

marched to the steps of the *Union Leader* headquarters and began to refute Loeb's attacks on himself and his wife. But in the middle of the speech, Muskie, overwhelmed by emotion, broke down and cried. From that moment on, his ratings began to slip in the polls. Editor Loeb accused Muskie of being "near hysterical" and added: "A man with such emotions should not have his finger on the nuclear button."

1) What is your reaction to the apparent loss of public support that Muskie suffered after this incident?

2) Would you vote for a candidate if you knew that he or she had

a) lost their temper in a political debate?

b) been arrested once for drunken driving?

c) consulted a psychiatrist?

d) divorced their spouse?

e) abandoned their religious affiliations?

Give reasons for your answers.

3) Check your list with others in your class. Judging from the class responses, what expectations do people have of the personal lives of candidates? Are such expectations justified in your opinion?

The Sting of Criticism

Harry Truman once advised politicians: "If you can't stand the heat, stay out of the kitchen." Some elected officials—especially on local and state levels—have taken his advice because the caustic criticisms of political opponents and the suspicions of an ill-informed public have touched their own families or wounded their sense of personal worth. To prevent the give-and-take of political debate from degenerating into personal attacks and mudslinging is a constant challenge for those engaged in the art of politics. Apparently, the failures in this area have led to disillusionment for many competent officeholders.

Examine the following fictional case of the state legislator who faces what he considers unfair charges of "a conflict of interests."

An Honest Man Smeared

Leon Walker is a senior partner in the legal firm of Dean, Walker, Thompson, and Redlund. Among the firm's clients are several land developers and real estate firms.

Walker is a member of the state legislature and was recently appointed to a special committee to study and develop land-use legislation. Walker was selected for the committee because of his special expertise on the subject and his reputation for honesty and integrity. Walker initially turned down the assignment because he felt others might feel a potential conflict of interest existed because of his firm's legal business and land-use legislation which might be proposed. Walker accepted the assignment only after publicly disclosing his firm's ties to the land developers and real estate interests. In addition, he made public his personal tax records for the past ten years. Walker also disclosed his campaign contributors and has refused to accept contributions from developers or others who might be affected by the land-use legislation.

Now Walker is running for re-election and his opponent is charging him with a conflict of interest. "How," says his opponent, "can Walker vote on land-use legislation if his firm does business with those who will be affected by the new laws? This is a serious breach of ethics, and Walker should either resign from the legislature or resign from his law firm."

Walker, who takes a great deal of pride in his eight-year legislative record, is incensed by the charges. "No one questioned my honesty before," he says. "Yesterday my son came home from school crying because someone said they'd read in the papers that his dad was a crook. If I go to the super-market, I think people are pointing at me.

My opponent isn't bothering to distinguish between a potential conflict and a real one.

"If I wasn't aware of the potential conflict, I wouldn't have disclosed. I didn't have to; there's no law. As a public official, I have to expect criticism, but when criticism affects your family, that's too much. Frankly, I'd like to get out of politics."

1) What is the difference between a real conflict of interest and a potential conflict?

2) Do you think Walker's opponent is raising a legitimate issue? Why or why not?

3) If you were in Walker's place, what choices would you have? What would be the consequences of each? What would you decide and why?

4) Would you quit if you couldn't be cleared of the smear charges? Why or why not?

The Painful Pressures

The emotional strain placed upon those who hold public office is tremendous. Campaigns and legislative sessions are both emotionally and physically exhausting. Tensions arise, the pace quickens, the days become longer and more tiring. For many candidates, legislators and other elected officials, eighteen- and twenty-hour days often are the norm. Furthermore, politics is, by its nature, controversial. People must choose sides and often become angry or frustrated in the face of opposition. This accumulation of tension may put undue stress on a person's physical and psychic resources.

Read the following description of the day in the life of a presidential candidate. How does this passage make you feel?

Meet the Candidate!

"You must emerge, bright and bubbling with wisdom and well-being, every morning at 8 o'clock, just in time for a charming and profound breakfast talk, shake hands with hundreds, often literally thousands, of people, make several inspiring, "newsworthy" speeches during the day, confer with political leaders along the way and with your staff all the time, write at every chance, think, if possible, read mail and newspapers, talk on the telephone, talk to everybody, dictate, receive delegations, eat with decorum—and discretion!—and ride through city after city on the back of an open car, smiling until your mouth is dehydrated by the wind, waving until the blood runs out of your arm, and then bounce gaily, confidently, masterfully into great hallowing halls, shaved and all made up for television with the right color shirt and tie—I always forgot—and a manuscript so defaced with chicken tracks and last-minute jottings that you couldn't follow it, even if the spotlights weren't blinding you and even if the still photographers didn't shoot you in the eye every time you looked at them. Then all you have to do is make a great, imperishable speech, get out through the pressing crowds with a few score autographs, your clothes intact, your hands bruised, and back to the hotel—in time to see a few important people."

Adlai Stevenson

Shortly after Senator Walter Mondale of Minnesota decided in the fall of 1974 not to run for the presidency, he explained to the press why he had lost interest in making the race:

"The absolutely unbelievable schedules, the eighteen-hour days, the weekends. Above all, there's no time to sit down and think

through an issue, to read books and other things you should, to test and probe an idea to be sure you're on the right track, to talk with leaders in the field. That has always been my way. I'm just uncomfortable with the snap judgments that one makes when you're tired or don't have a chance to think things through."

Minneapolis Tribune

Is there any way out of Senator Mondale's dilemma for someone who aspires to run for the presidency of the United States, in your opinion? Explain.

The Risk of Defeat

Most politicians need a higher degree of self confidence and self esteem than the public at large. Most of us want and actively seek a certain amount of approval and recognition, but by asking for the votes of large numbers of people, a political candidate asks for recognition on a much wider scale.

To spend the time, the money, and to make the sacrifices which all candidates make, only to be defeated and rejected by those whose approval you sought, requires a great deal of emotional preparation. It is a difficult but necessary personal price. Here is how one politician reflected on his experience of political defeats:

"No one likes to lose . . . It hardly qualifies as fun. But when you run for office, you accept defeat as one of the risks. I've never felt personally rejected. After all, a great many people voted for me, in fact, almost as many as voted for my opponent.

"There are other factors that compensate for the defeat. In my first loss, I almost won against huge odds. There was a landslide all over the state for the other party. Candidates of my party were submerged. In losing by only a few votes, I led my party's ticket. I probably received more glory in defeat than I would have in victory. My political stock rose all over the state.

"My next defeat was something else. I was deeply hurt. I haven't gotten over it entirely two years later. The political situation in the state had stabilized itself and my party was on the upswing. I ran an excellent campaign and fully expected to win. I lost because of a situation in one of the towns of my district. I was not involved in any way, but I went down in defeat because of it. The mayor of the town was a member of my party and an excellent man. He took a courageous but unpopular stand on a local issue—it doesn't matter what it was. Personally, I felt he was right. It was a matter of principle and in his situation I might have done the same. But the result was a big vote against him and the party in that town, which offset the margin I had built up elsewhere in the district. I still ran at the top of the ticket, but not by as much. It hurt to have lost not by my own doing and over a purely emotional issue."

Robert Liston

1) Have you ever chosen to avoid a competitive situation because you feared defeat? How do you evaluate your choice now?

2) What are the possible benefits that a politician might gain from defeat in an election?

3) What are the value conflicts between the "New Politics" which sees a good in "a moral victory" and the "Old Politics" which sees being out of office as the worst possible evil? Which of these views would you agree with?

4) How would you react to helping in a political campaign where the result is almost certainly defeat?

The Financial Dilemma

Holding public office is for many a financial burden. George Washington Plunkitt may not have considered that to be the case, but we are many years removed from Tammany Hall. The days of what Plunkitt considered "honest graft" are long behind us. Our political system has lost a great many talented and gifted individuals who left politics for no other reason than the financial burdens it imposed upon them.

1) Find out what the elected members of your school board are paid, your city council, your local mayor, and your state legislators. Do you think their salaries are enough? Try to find out how many hours they put in each month. Would you work for that?

2) Do you think the pay most public officials receive excludes certain occupational classes from holding public office? What other factors would exclude people from holding office?

Consider the following fictional case:

Porter's Complaint

Representative Thomas Porter, an attorney with a large law firm, has served in the state legislature for eight years. He is 38, married, and the father of three school-age children. Popular with his colleagues, Porter is an extremely effective legislator and is considered a sure bet for reelection.

Porter spends three to five months each year in the state capital while the legislature is in session. When the legislature is not in session, he must commute once or twice a week to attend committee meetings or take care of other business.

On a yearly basis, Porter's legislative duties take up about 60-75 percent of his time. He receives about $5,000 because of the limited amount of time he can devote to legal work.

"Most attorneys," he says, "at my age and with my experience, earn between $25,000 and $30,000. My income last year was just over $14,000. Two of my kids will start college soon and I can't afford to send them on that kind of money.

"I love the legislature," he said, "I think I've done a lot of good there, but it's to the point where I have to choose between earning a living and serving the people."

1) What is the value conflict here?

2) If you were in Porter's position, what choice would you make?

3) How would you arrive at your decision?

The Problem of Compromise

"Once, at a Tammany Fourth of July cele-
bration, a reporter wondered and later asked
why Mr. Charles F. Murphy (he was always
Mister even to his closest associates) did not
join in the singing of the National Anthem.
"'Perhaps he didn't want to commit himself,' the boss's aide explained."

Arthur Mann

Almost every politician wants to do the
right thing. Often it's hard to know what's
right and sometimes the decision may be
difficult. At other times, the right course
of action may be practically impossible or
the costs of acting that way may far outweigh whatever advantages are gained. Almost all politicians have had compromise
suggested at some point in their careers.

The politician, like every other member of
our society, must consider the consequences
of non-compromise: probable defeat at the
polls. Politicians do not like to admit alter-
ing their views, even slightly, to win the
support of powerful labor unions, business
groups, or political parties, but many of
them do. And just as most people do not go
out of their way to alienate the boss when a
pay raise is due, most politicians do not go
out of their way to alienate voters around
election time.

This fictional case illustrates the problems
involved:

Politics and Principles

As a candidate for state legislature, your
campaign committee is meeting to determine how you will handle the controversial
issues that are sure to surface during the
campaign.

Abortion reform and gun control have
been raised by your opponent during your
joint debates as two issues that clearly divide the two of you. She is in favor of a
strong anti-abortion law and is against any
form of gun control. You, on the other hand,
have no strong feelings on abortion but do
feel that handguns ought to be registered.

The make-up of your district is heavily
Catholic and generally anti-abortion. A
recent poll also indicates that 53 percent of
your district is opposed to any form of gun
control.

As the debate goes on in the committee,
several courses of action become clear. Here
are your alternatives:

1) You can come down strongly against
abortion and blunt that issue, even though
you personally have some qualms about that
position.

2) You can totally ignore both issues and avoid the conflict.

3) You can come out in favor of a strong anti-abortion law and ignore the issue of gun control, thus creating a "smoke screen" to avoid the consequences of taking a strong stand on gun control.

4) You can state your position on both issues and take your chances.

Which of the above positions are you most comfortable with personally and why? Is there perhaps another way of handling the situation than the alternatives presented by the committee?

Summary Exercise

Here is a list of the personal costs involved in running for a political office. Add any others to the list that you consider important. Then rank order the items on the list placing number one after the item you consider the most difficult and then scaling the others according to their relative importance.

Conflict with time
The loss of privacy
Physical and/or emotional stress
Financial loss
The prospect of criticism
The risk of defeat
The need for compromise

1) What does your list reveal about your own values?

2) Do you consider any of these costs too high? If so, can you recommend some changes in campaign practices which might make running for election less difficult?

3) Do you feel that the benefits of gaining a political office outweigh the difficulties involved? Why or why not?

SENSITIVITY MODULES:
Discovering and Expressing

1) Select a candidate for political office from the national, state, or local scene in whom you are interested. Learn as much as you can about this person. Then make a collage on the theme, "Portrait of a Candidate," in which you introduce your class to this candidate.

2) Have some representative from your class arrange to interview the spouse of a candidate. Discuss with the person you interview what he or she feels are the rewards and costs of running for political office. Be sure to find out how the candidate made the decision to get into politics, how that decision has affected the family, and whether the struggle has been worth it from the spouse's viewpoint. Let this representative report on the interview to the class.

3) Get a list of all the representatives in your state legislature or assembly. Find out what each member's occupation or profession is. Are some occupations more heavily represented than others? Given the time and money involved, do you believe that people in any trade or profession can aspire to public office? Discuss the implications of your survey with other members of your class.

4) Write a letter addressed to a staff person of a national congressional representative. Ask for a copy of the politician's monthly calendar for any one of the three months preceding the last election. What percentage of time does this politician spend campaigning?

Suggested Readings

Barone, M., Ujifusa, G. and Mathews, D. *The Almanac of American Politics*. Boston: Gambit, 1974. A detailed analysis of the politics of every state and congressional district in the United States.

Campaign Insight: An Overview of Political Techniques. (A biweekly newsletter published by Campaign Associates, Inc., 408 Petroleum Building, Wichita, Kansas 67202.) A "must" for persons interested in political candidates and campaigns.

Hoopes, Roy. *Getting With Politics: A Guide to Political Action for Young People*. Paperback ed. New York: Dell, 1968. A bipartisan look at political activity.

Lee, Richard W., ed. *Politics and the Press*. Paperback ed. Washington, D.C.: Acropolis Books, 1970. An analysis of television and press coverage of politics and of public opinion polling.

Lindsay, John. *Journey Into Politics*. New York: Dodd, Mead, 1967. Interesting views of the former mayor of New York.

THE CAMPAIGN

The Will to Win

American political campaigns have a colorful history: whistlestop train caravans, catchy songs and ditties, rhymed slogans like "Tippecanoe and Tyler Too," and more recently, scores of journalists jetting across the country with presidential candidates.

In 1972, young people clapped their hands to the McGovern version of "This Land Is Your Land." In the mid 1960's, people sang "Hello Lyndon" to the tune of "Hello Dolly"; and in the Depression years, young and old alike responded to Franklin D. Roosevelt's campaign song "Happy Days Are Here Again." Traditionally, Americans like spirited political campaigns; sometimes campaigns even become celebrations of what Americans value most about their country.

The campaign tradition in America, however, has a dark side as well: mud-slinging tactics, whispering campaigns, unfounded charges, and "dirty tricks" bordering on the unethical. A basic issue that underlies all campaign practices is: In a good political cause, should a candidate attempt to win *by any means* available? Is "dirty politics" ever justified? The recent Watergate tragedy stresses the importance of these questions.

This chapter will deal with the practical and basic questions about a political campaign. How should a campaign be run? What is the importance of issues and arguments? Of strategies and tactics? What should be the content of a good and effective campaign? How do local and state campaigns differ from national campaigns? Before we can deal with these central questions, however, we must deal with this immediate problem: How important is winning? The issue is not exclusively a political one. The following quotations highlight contrasting views of competition in American sports.

**When the One Great Scorer
Comes to write against your name,
He writes not that you won or lost
But how you played the game.**
Grantland Rice (Sportswriter, 1923)

"Winning isn't everything. It's the only thing."
Vince Lombardi (Football coach, 1960)

Candidates who decide to run for political office must choose one of these positions. Is "winning the only thing," as Lombardi said? Or is playing a good game what counts?

We can analyze these questions and find solid reasons to support either view. Certainly we need candidates who are willing to run even in a losing struggle, to give voice to deeply held convictions that the American public may have lost sight of.

On the other hand, "What's the point of raising hell," as John Kennedy once said, "unless you can win?" He had been taught that politics is not the place to score moral points but to win and, after one had won, to work for reform and justice.

There's nothing wrong with competition or with winning in itself. When people achieve promotions, awards, scholarships or fellowships and the like, it means that society is going to aid its most capable members to assume responsible positions on the basis of merit and accomplishment. However, when competition means winning at any cost, it provokes rightful criticism.

But we should remember that competition —if fair and well-motivated—can result in quality work in the professions and better performance in our political institutions. When the work of capable people is rewarded on the basis of honest competition, mediocrity and "time serving" can be reduced in many of our corporations and government agencies. "Winning" can have many beneficial effects in a society.

In this chapter we are going to assume that a candidate believes in what he or she is doing and is willing to fight hard to win. Given that assumption, the next question is how does a candidate conduct a fair campaign.

Winning the Endorsement

Whenever a person wants to embark on a profession, apply for a job, or enter college, he or she must provide references or letters of recommendation. Every graduating high school senior faces the question of whom to ask for these kinds of endorsement. The kind of future the graduate aspires to will weigh heavily on the kind of references he or she can offer.

What are the references? Where do you get them? Whom would you ask for a reference? What are the references used for?

After you have thought about these questions, compile a list of people whom you would feel comfortable in using as references. Why did you list each of these persons? How do you think your future employer or counselor might view these names? How important do you think it is to use "respected" people as references?

Party Endorsement

Having people who can vouch for you is one way of succeeding in our society. This is particularly true in the political arena. The term for political references is *endorsements*. Political candidates and their campaign organizations work to find prominent citizens or prestigious groups to speak on their behalf. Candidates realize that voters who know little about the persons running for an office will judge them by the people who endorse them, and vote accordingly.

Political parties set up screening and endorsement committees to weed out weaker candidates. These committees make it easier for conventions to endorse a candidate who can win, and who can represent the party's goals as well. Usually, party endorsement gives a candidate valuable benefits: money, campaign workers, and a definite voter base. Many party members will cooperate with a candidate they don't know well simply on the basis of party endorsement.

Party conventions often face painful and difficult choices. Endorsing a promising newcomer who is not the choice of "party regulars" may lead to a primary fight that can split the party. Or party activists may not reflect the thinking of the mass of voters and they may endorse a candidate who cannot win.

Examine the following three fictional cases that highlight some problems for a candidate who is seeking endorsement or for a party that has to make one.

A Candidate's Compromise

Lance Whitman lives in a state where the average age of a congressional representative is fifty-five. Lance feels strongly that many of these older legislators are tied to the interests of large business corporations and they do not pay enough attention to the problems of small business people.

Lance is twenty-eight. After graduating from a local agricultural college, he went into partnership with his father as a dairy farmer. Lance and his father have always been active in politics, and some people in the party have convinced Lance that he should seek party endorsement and campaign for the vacant seat in the House.

In Lance's district, the party is controlled by pro-labor forces. A majority of the working people in the district are employed by "Milkmaid, Inc."—one of the largest dairy corporations in the state. The corporation wants to expand and build a new cheese processing plant in Lance's town. Many of the townspeople are in favor of the move since the new construction would bring more jobs to the area and improve the standard of living. However, "Milkmaid" wants to buy out some of the individual dairy farms and incorporate these into the company. Lance, his family, and his friends are strongly opposed to this action since they want to preserve individual ownership of farms.

But Lance knows that the support of the labor union group is crucial to winning the party's endorsement; therefore, he decides to come out in favor of the corporation's interest. He explains privately to his friends and supporters that, once elected, he will be in a position to vote the way he pleases, and so this initial compromise is necessary.

1) Do you agree or disagree with Lance's position? Explain your answer in terms of the conflicting values.

2) Can you think of any other alternatives that Lance might choose? How effective might these be?

Three to Get Ready

When the delegates from the 44th district met at their local convention, they knew that they would face some tough decisions over endorsement. The district they represented had a liberal voting record and it consisted of a large university population with an interesting balance of working class and professional people. In recent years the liberal wing of the party successfully united these groups, and now this coalition comprises 60 percent of the total delegates.

A symbol of these earlier struggles is a liberal-minded lawyer, Wilson Grange. While serving as campaign manager for a progressive candidate in the last election he gained the support of such diverse groups as the women's caucus, the black militant groups and the local labor unions. Wilson evokes strong feelings of friendship and loyalty among all the delegates.

A new contender on the political scene is Mary Kowalski. In her job as Director of Human Services, she has shown effective administrative abilities. Although she is sympathetic to women's issues and to minority struggles, Mary takes a middle-of-the-road approach to controversial issues. Mary, like Wilson, already has a strong campaign organization.

Sonny Jackson, a community organizer, is also seeking the endorsement. As a black candidate, he has the support of some groups who want more political representation for minorities. However, Sonny has little party strength nor does he have the support of all the blacks in the community—some of whom are uncomfortable with his militancy.

The women delegates comprise forty-five percent of the convention. They would like to see a woman elected to state office. Most of them, in the past, supported Wilson Grange. Minority groups, in general, favor Sonny Jackson. However, if they vote for Wilson Grange, he might have more power to get the kind of legislation they favor.

Group Exercise: Divide the class into three groups. Forty-five percent should play the women at the convention; 10 percent of the class should represent the minority groups, and the remainder should represent the men. Choose some members of the class to act as floor managers for each of the candidates and to move in and out of the various caucuses trying to get majority support for their candidate. After twenty minutes, poll the individuals in the class and give the results of the vote.

The Party Picks a Winner

One issue that concerns every citizen in Allenwood is the rapid increase of crime in the city. Statistics show that the crime rate has risen nine percent in the past year. The people tend to blame the incumbent mayor, a Democrat, for lack of leadership in enforcing the law. The Republicans feel confident that whomever they endorse as the mayoral candidate can win.

Two Republicans are seeking the party endorsement. Mike Rossi is a lawyer who has worked in the city attorney's office, and he is running on a tough "no-nonsense" platform. He is strong on law and order but not always sensitive to civil liberties. Rossi has built up an effective campaign organization and already has a broad base of support among working-class Republicans, influential Democrats, and a large number of Independents.

Dan Miles is the director of the County Welfare Department, and he has won national recognition for his social service reforms. Miles feels that sensitizing the police force to the needs of the poor, minorities, and women would have a significant effect in reducing the crime rate. Dan draws his active support from the local chapter of the Ripon Society, a liberal wing of the Republican party.

At the convention, Dan Miles exercises persuasive leadership. The majority of the delegates feel that Miles' proposals for reform are much more substantial than Rossi's. But, at the same time, the delegates realize that Rossi has an impressive lead among the voters. His campaign managers remind the party that if Rossi fails to win the endorsement, he would run in the primary and he might win without the party's endorsement. The resulting split might favor the Democratic candidate.

1) If you were one of the delegates who favored Miles, how would you vote?

2) Find a classmate who would vote differently than you and listen to his or her arguments. Explain your own position.

Individual Endorsement

Besides the party's endorsement, every candidate wants the support of prominent citizens who have some standing in the community. In politics the old adage "a man is known by the company he keeps" is especially true. People who do not know a candidate personally may vote for him or her on the basis of others' recommendations. The question then becomes: Whose endorsement should be sought?

In the following exercise remember that you as a candidate are attempting to influence people's judgment through the use of another's credibility.

Who Goes in the Ad?

You are running for the Adams County Board of Supervisors. Your district is heavily conservative with a large proportion of Lutherans—mostly of German descent. A number of people in the district have volunteered to let you use their name in an endorsement ad to be run in the local newspaper. The ad will be run shortly before the election.

Which names would you not use and why not? What criteria do you use in making your selections? How would your choices change if your district was very liberal?

Dan Schmidt: Dan is a man who likes his liquor and loves politics. He spends most of his nights in Maxie's Pub where a number of other men gather to drink beer and talk.

Dan is a popular fellow and many of his fellow drinkers rely heavily on Dan's advice where politics is concerned. Despite his drinking problem, he is well-informed on issues and candidates.

Jack Singer: Jack is the mayor of the largest town in your district. He has never lost an election. His wife recently divorced him and won custody of the children after a long and bitter court fight. Jack has told you privately that he intends to resign as mayor in the near future.

Jim Whitlaw: Jim is the president of the local teachers' union and recently led a successful teacher strike which resulted in a twenty percent increase in faculty salaries. All three schools in town were closed for several weeks. The strike was highly divisive in the district with about half the people supporting the teachers and the rest supporting the administration.

Harry Rutkowski: Harry has been a lineman with the telephone company for eighteen years. While he disagrees with many of your views, he has agreed to support you because you live in his neighborhood and belong to the same church. Harry is not well-known in the community.

TAMMANANNY, *A GROSS BLOW* has befallen **POGO'S CANDIDATURE**

HE'S MADE A SPEECH?

NO, he was mixed up with some *COWBIRDS!* The Deacon claims it *Blackens* POGO'S name ☞

SOMEONE MUST ENDORSE POGO'S CHARACTER!

YES! It will take a man of ☞ **PROVEN** *MERIT!* A CITIZEN WHO *TOWERS* ABOVE THE CROWD. ★★ A FIGURE ADMIRED *and* BELOVED *by ALL !!!*

IT'LL BE HARD TO GET SUCH A MAN TO SPEAK UP AND RISK HIS *OWN* GOOD NAME.

SAY NOT *SO!!* These are TIMES *for* ☞ *STALWARCY & PLUCK* ☜ One noble soul must risk it ╌ I, P.T. BRIDGEPORT *WILL SPEAK FOR POGO!!*

YOU SURE THAT FIGURE IS UNIVERSALLY ADMIRED?

Janet Meyers: Janet is the head of a local church women's society and is very conservative. She is an aggressive spokeswoman for the more reactionary groups in town. She has championed "law and order" causes and recently led a fight to close down a local movie theatre which was showing X-rated films.

Bill Kant: Bill is an attorney for the American Civil Liberties Union and is a close personal friend of yours who has offered his earnest support. Bill is very liberal and two years ago supported a candidate of the Socialist Workers Party for the state legislature. You know that by adding Bill's name you will lose more votes than you will gain.

Dealing with the Opponent

"Charge what they can't deny, and deny what they're not charging."

Murray Chotiner, long-time political adviser to Richard Nixon

Every challenger in the political arena faces a perplexing dilemma. Everyone likes a "nice guy," and the public reacts unfavorably to aggressive attacks on political foes. Yet if you can't demonstrate a genuine contrast between yourself and the incumbent, how will the voters know that they have a real *choice*? It's much easier for the incumbent to adopt a pleasant style because he can point to his record (unless it's terrible), and he already has a head start in voter identification.

Professional "pols" generally agree that there are four basic strategies for dealing with an opponent in a campaign:

a) Ignore your opponent; promote your own assets.
b) Focus attention on your opponent's record.
c) Attack your opponent's personal life or qualities.
d) Debate your opponent directly.

1) How would each of these strategies look if you were an incumbent? a challenger?

2) Would you consider any one of these strategies unfair or unethical? Give the reasons for your answer.

3) Are there any circumstances in which you would use an "unfair" strategy? Why or why not?

Analyze what strategy is used in each of these cases and explain which strategies you could not justify.

1) Incumbent Fred Rockingham, state treasurer, attacks his challenger Joan La Follette's qualifications because he claims that, in a period of high inflation combined with recession, "women aren't good at managing money." If you were Rockingham's campaign advisor, would you support this kind of attack? Explain.

2) Cissy Adams, reform candidate for the national House of Representatives in a southern state, blisters veteran congressman Rhett Fox because he has divorced his wife of thirty years and taken up with a twenty-four year old political reporter for *Sisterhood*, a feminist magazine. Should Ms. Adams continue to criticize Fox's private life in her campaign? Why?

3) Millionaire Guy Rathskeller, governor of a large midwestern state, secretly agrees to hire a private detective agency to delve into the private life of his challenger Sam Vitale. Rathskeller knows that Vitale's first wife divorced him five years ago. If you were Rathskeller, would you use any information related to the divorce case in your campaign? Why or why not?

4) John LaTouche, challenger in a national senatorial race in a large state, faces a popular incumbent—Senator Andy Godbout. LaTouche's entire campaign attack is to charge Brick White, Godbout's chief aide, with falsifying corporate tax returns a decade ago when White owned a snowmobile manufacturing company—Timber Wolf Enterprises, Inc. A week before the election, LaTouche is given certain proof that Brick White did not falsify his tax returns. Should LaTouche make this information public? Why? Why not?

5) Elliot Goodman, campaign manager for an incumbent senator, hires a former secretary in his own firm, Campaign Trailblazers, Inc., to pose as a supporter of the challenger Tom Meany. She is to accept a secretary's job in Meany's campaign office, but her real mission is to pass on information about Meany's campaign to her old boss. If you were in the secretary's position, would you accept this assignment? Why?

6) Senator Mabel Wiley, a veteran of twelve years in Congress, faces a very stiff primary challenge from Steve O'Brien, a bright young lawyer who is charging her with being "The Lady Senator from Atlas Oil." Mabel has consistently supported the oil depletion allowance. Her campaign organization advises her to hire a team of "dirty tricksters" to circulate literature accusing O'Brien of being a "socialist" and "an enemy of free enterprise." Should she accept their advice? Why or why not?

7) Representative Jed Frye is being challenged by Professor Irving Hecht, an economist, in the general election. Hecht invites Frye to defend in public debate his votes on tax reform and other sensitive economic issues. Frye refuses to debate, stays in Washington for most of the campaign, and returns home a week before election day for a "whirlwind campaign" of his district. Frye believes in a "nice guy approach" to campaigning. If you were Frye, would you have avoided a public debate? Why or why not?

The following two cases highlight some problems in deciding how to deal with an opponent. Imagine that you are the campaign manager in each case. What strategy would you propose to your candidate? Justify your choice.

Truth and Consequences

Your candidate lives in a district where a hotly contested primary election campaign is being waged. While soliciting money one day you run into a friend who tells you that the other candidate of your party did not register for the draft during the Vietnam War and that there may be a federal warrant still outstanding.

This is not public knowledge, and because of the powerful influence of the American Legion and the Veterans of Foreign Wars in your district, you know this information would seriously damage your opponent's campaign. Your problem is that you are convinced that these facts are irrelevant to the campaign.

Should you publicly reveal your opponent's problem and by so doing strengthen your candidate's position? Should you tell your candidate what you know and let him decide? Or do you say nothing and hope your candidate wins? What other options do you have?

"Man of the Year"

Pine River's incumbent mayor has served two terms and everyone in town knows him by sight. He is a friendly individual, out-going and gregarious; most people like him.

His political performance, however, is spotty. You and your candidate know and can prove that he has missed several council meetings without reason. He has a considerable drinking problem which most people in town choose to ignore. On one occasion the Mayor, after several drinks, insulted the president of a company which was thinking of building a plant in Pine River. Needless to say, the company located elsewhere. Unemployment in Pine River has risen to 8.5 percent.

The Mayor was recently honored by the American Legion as its "Man of the Year," and has served three years as Chairman of Pine River's Carnival Committee.

You feel very strongly that in spite of the mayor's personal popularity, he does not provide the leadership necessary to put Pine River back on its economic feet. You feel that your candidate can provide that leadership, and that the mayor should be defeated.

1) In attacking the mayor's lack of leadership, how would you handle the question of his excessive drinking? Would you ignore it, hint at it or refer to it directly? Explain.

2) As a campaign manager, what personal values that you hold firmly are in conflict in this campaign? How would you resolve the conflict so as to serve your candidate best?

Financing the Campaign

In their manual, *Tips on Political Fund Raising*, Campaign Associates, Inc. observes: "Running a political campaign without money is like trying to perform open-heart surgery with a pair of hedge clippers and no anesthetic—impossible! . . . While the presidential campaigns receive the most publicity, it is not unheard of for candidates to spend in excess of $100,000 for a low-paying city commission seat."

In Teddy Roosevelt's day, campaigns could be run on a modest budget because the old-time oratory was vigorous but inexpensive. With the advent of radio, costs began to climb. Television has brought with it teams of advertising and communication specialists, and expenditures have soared.

In 1974, candidates from both parties spent a whopping eighty million dollars in the national congressional races: 45 million for the Democrats, 35 million for the Republicans. The increasing number of eligible voters (that is, eighteen to twenty-one year olds) has added more to the cost of reaching all the voters.

Twenty percent of the 1974 contributions poured in from "special interests": professional associations, labor unions, business groups, public interest groups, etc. With the shift from individual wealthy donors to group resources (television reporter Dan Rather says "the fat cats now travel in packs"), an obvious problem for the candidate is how to finance a campaign and yet remain free from control by big contributors.

Costs of the Campaign

Imagine that a twenty-one-year-old alumnus of your school, Fred Krupsak, decides to run for the state legislature from your district and asks your class to staff his campaign organization. He has raised $4,000 from party and other sources for the campaign, and your class is asked to decide how he can best use these funds for public relations and advertising.

Fred estimates that he will need $1,500 of the $4,000 for headquarters expense, campaign activities (rallies, motorcades, travel, etc.). The number of voters in Fred's district is 28,000, and he has been told by campaign professionals that he will need at least 7,000 pieces of basic literature.

Have groups in your class investigate the costs of the following public relations and advertising media and make a budget estimate.

	Quantity	Total Cost
Brochures	7,000	$ _____
Letterhead stationery	2,000	_____
Reminder postcards	2,000	_____
Handout cards	7,000	_____
Bumper stickers	500	_____
Yard signs	750	_____
Buttons	500	_____
Outdoor billboards	3	_____
Radio spots: 30 seconds	1 in prime time on largest metro station	_____
TV spots: 30 seconds	1 in prime time on largest metro channel	_____
Newspaper ads: half-page	4 in big daily 2 each in two weeklies	_____
Photos of candidate	4 (for brochure)	_____
Postage for brochures, letters, postcards	12,000 first class mailings	_____

1) What items would you give first priority? Why?

2) Which would you eliminate? Remember, $2500 is your spending limit.

3) How did you determine which media to use?

4) Bring together all the estimated costs, discuss and decide priorities, and prepare a budget for submission to Fred Krupsak.

Raising Campaign Funds

Once a candidate has determined how much money he or she needs to conduct a campaign, the big question remains: How is it to be raised? Fundraising is the most difficult part of a political campaign. In most areas candidates set up financial committees to assist in raising money.

These fundraising operations usually are legally separated from the candidate. This is done in order that the candidate will not be legally responsible for campaign activities or personally responsible for campaign debts. Large corporations use similar methods to avoid being legally responsible for their subsidiaries in the event of bankruptcy, etc.

If the candidate is not legally responsible, he or she *is* morally responsible. The candidate still must decide from whom to solicit money and from whom not to accept it.

The problem a candidate faces is that the major source of campaign funding comes from those who have an interest in the office being sought: corporation board members, labor union officials, small businessmen, building contractors, and the like. The question each candidate for political office must ask is whether or not a financial contribution from an individual or group would tend to influence his or her decisions while in office.

Should candidates for political office refuse under any circumstances to accept money from those who have a vested interest in the office? Would it change your decision if you knew that those who adopt that philosophy usually lose elections for lack of funds?

Deciding on Donors

You are a candidate for Mayor of Nonantum, a town of 80,000. You have not run for office previously but have been active in a number of campaigns. Your campaign budget is $19,500, and you have raised about $3,000 from your personal funds and contributions from close friends. You are convinced that the only way you can win is to raise the entire $16,500 called for by the budget. The following groups and individuals have volunteered to contribute to your campaign.

Fred Kelly: Fred is the state chairman

of your political party. You do not know Fred very well but he always contributes to candidates of his party. That's how Fred remains state party chairman. Fred has offered you $200. Would you accept the money? Why?

Lester Murdock: Lester is the state senator from your district. You like Lester personally but he belongs to the other party. Many people think your candidacy for mayor is a jumping off point for an eventual run against Lester. You've thought about it also and you're certain that Lester's $350 offer is meant to persuade you not to run against him. Would you accept his contribution? Why?

Joe Morton: Joe is the head of the city planning department. If Joe is to keep his job, he must be reappointed by the new mayor. State law forbids civil service employees from contributing to political campaigns. Joe says not to worry about that; he'll have his wife or brother send you $50. You learn that Joe also contributed to your opponent. Would you accept his donation? Why?

Peter D'Antonio: Pete is an attorney and also your best friend. Pete is more or less running your campaign and has just offered to put $1,500 of his own money into it. A mutual friend has just told you that Pete has a burning desire to be city attorney although Pete has never mentioned it to you. The mayor appoints the city attorney. Would you accept Pete's contribution? Why?

Abe Clinton: Abe is the business agent for the very powerful Teamsters Union, which represents most of the city employees, and you know that you will be dealing directly with Abe in bargaining contracts if you are elected. As a former member of the Teamsters, you have many friends in the union. You consider yourself "labor-oriented." Abe has offered to send you $2,500 for your campaign from Teamsters' political funds. Would you accept? Why?

Emery Bergstrom: Emery is president and majority stockholder in the Swan River Power Company. S.R.P. is the sole source of electrical power in your community. State law gives the mayor the authority to appoint a special commission to set electrical rates. Emery has offered to send you a check for $3,000. Would you accept his gift? Why?

Marvin Johnson: Marvin is the executive secretary of the local chamber of commerce. He has told you that several businessmen would like to contribute $500 to your cam-

paign but are afraid it would hurt business if that information were made public. Marvin has said he'll collect the money and give it to you so you won't have to worry or know where it came from. Would you accept this money? Why?

1) What criteria would you suggest as a means of making judgments in these situations?

2) Compare your criteria with those of your classmates.

When Money Runs Out

As a candidate for city council, you have budgeted $14,000 for your campaign. Despite the fact that you have been endorsed by the Republican Party and received the political support of the local chamber of commerce, only $3,400 has thus far been contributed to your campaign. With less than a month to go, you call a meeting of your campaign committee to discuss the situation. The following alternatives are suggested:

1) You promised when you started the campaign to reveal all your contributors. This has led a few major contributors to Republican causes to either refrain completely or cut back considerably on their contributions. The suggestion is that you abandon your early campaign promise and reveal only the names of the persons who want their contributions revealed.

2) An obvious solution is to cut way back on campaign expenditures and live within the $3,400 collected.

3) Another suggestion is to contact personally known large contributors to explain your plight and to solicit enough money to keep the campaign going.

4) Several committee members feel the most beneficial way of handling the problem is to hold general fundraisers open to everyone: cocktail parties, dinners, dances, raffles, etc.

1) Which of these would you reject on ethical grounds? Why?

2) Which strategy would you then favor? Why?

3) Can you suggest any other alternatives? Explain.

A Case of Corporate Aid

As fundraising chairman for a congressional candidate, you are responsible for raising the money to pay for the campaign. To date you have raised about $50,000 or about two-thirds of your budget.

The election is three weeks away and the campaign is desperately in need of money.

You'll need at least $10,000 to pay for television time in the remaining weeks, some of the campaign workers need to be paid, and the last minute mailing to voters will cost about $10,000.

Your candidate is running a tight, clean, and open campaign, sticking to the issues and ignoring the opponent, a twenty-six year incumbent. The newspapers refer to your candidate as the "reform" candidate. The latest polls show your candidate trailing by only two percentage points.

You've just come from a meeting where it was made very clear to you that your candidate's only hope of winning rests with your ability to finance the remainder of the campaign.

You think you're in good shape. You've two more large fundraisers scheduled and it looks as if they'll bring in about $10,000. You've also got contributor pledges totaling almost $13,000, and while that leaves you just a few thousand short, you're confident that the remainder can easily be raised.

However, a newspaper article in the morning's paper disturbs you. Several executives of a large corporation in your state have been accused of making illegal campaign contributions to candidates in other states. Apparently they had made the contributions with personal funds and later were reimbursed with corporate funds.

A quick check of your records indicates that while the two corporate officers mentioned did not contribute to your campaign, other officers of the same corporation did. In fact, the total amount of their contributions was over $5,000.

Should you return the money and jeopardize your candidate's chances? What would you do?

Persuading the Voter

Creating an Image

In the history of politics candidates have always considered carefully how to persuade voters to support them. From the time of the ancient Greeks, experts in political persuasion have insisted on the need for the candidate to establish *ethos*—that is, a character and a personal style that the people trust. Certain American politicians in our past have had strong *ethos*: Abraham Lincoln, Andrew Jackson, Woodrow Wilson.

In the age of mass media—television, especially—the emphasis has shifted to *image making*, a form of ethos highly dependent on a friendly, relaxed TV style, an attractive face on the television screen, and a cool style of speaking adapted to television's intimate entrance into the nation's livingrooms. Some observers have raised questions about this new style of political persuasion: Does the "image" reveal or conceal the real person who is running for office? Is the TV-created "image" eliminating the *substance* of campaigns, that is, serious stands on vital issues? Is the modern campaign causing Americans to elect "personalities" to important offices rather than competent candidates who can govern or legislate effectively?

Consider the McGovern-Nixon presiden-

tial contest of 1972 and the Humphrey-Nixon race of 1968. What "image" did each candidate try to establish in 1972? in 1968? In your opinion, which of the candidates succeeded well in establishing the "image" he wanted the public to have? Was any can-

didate perceived by the public in 1968 or 1972 as having a different "image" than he wanted to convey? Explain. (Consult *The Making of a President* by Theodore H. White or *An American Melodrama* by Chester, Hodgson, and Page.) Consider these two fictional cases:

Watching Scotty Run

State legislator Scotty McGraw, a Democrat, decides to challenge the national senator from his state—Archibald Morton, a veteran moderate Republican. McGraw hires a "communications expert" to help him "get through" to the voters who, according to state-wide polls, are looking for fresh ideas and a new face.

The consultant wants McGraw to create a friendly image—the picture of a man who appeals to most segments of the voting public. But McGraw feels he is controversial; in the state legislature he took firm stands against nuclear power plants and other forms of industrial pollution. McGraw is a scrapper, and he thinks that he is at his best when he gives blunt, clearcut answers on difficult issues.

The consultant argues that the voters are tired of Senator Morton's outdated style. He urges McGraw to avoid sharp debate and a lot of specific stands on delicate issues. He maintains that if McGraw concentrates on being friendly with the voters and ignores Morton's lackluster record, he will ride on the current of change and be swept into office.

1) Do you think McGraw should follow the expert's advice? Why or why not?

2) What do you think of the expert's advice to avoid debate and specific stands? Is there any danger in this kind of advice—in your opinion? Explain.

A Question of Manipulation?

John Hirschberger has been a lawyer involved in many community activities: consumer protection groups, legal aid societies and the John Howard Society for prison reform. Last year John won the Democratic nomination for a national house seat from his congressional district; Steeltown, with a population of 450,000, is the key voting area in the district.

Hirschberger's campaign manager, "Red" Carter, knows that Steeltown is sports mad. Even though his candidate is not an ex-athletic star or even a sports enthusiast, Carter thinks that creating the image of John Hirschberger as an ardent sports fan is essential to winning votes from Democrats and independents in Steeltown. He hires a television producer to develop a series of thirty-second spots where Hirschberger will be shown shooting billiards in his cellar game room, snowmobiling with his children, and visiting the locker room of the local university football team.

Hirschberger doesn't think this approach reveals "the real person" at all, but Carter feels that emphasizing his candidate's work for prisoners and the poor won't have the vote-getting power of the "sports fan spots." The disagreement has split Hirschberger's campaign organization, and Hirschberger is losing ground in the polls against the Republican incumbent.

1) Should Hirschberger, in your opinion, "do his own thing" and fight for voter support on the basis of his actual record? Or should he accept Carter's strategy of appealing to the heavy sports fan vote?

2) What other strategic choices might Hirschberger have? Explain.

3) Why do campaign managers and media consultants often insist on a "sports image" for a political candidate? Do you see any connection between sports and politics? Explain.

4) Some observers would say that Carter's strategy is "manipulating the voters" and therefore dishonest. Do you agree or disagree? Why?

Dealing with the Issues

For many generations American voters have listened to great political debates and stirring speeches on basic issues in American life. The historic Lincoln-Douglas debates, William Jennings Bryan's attack on the gold standard, Franklin Roosevelt's call in 1932 for "a new deal," Lyndon Johnson's appeal for "a great society" in 1964: these are a few famous examples of effective political rhetoric. These speeches were marked by well-constructed arguments and a careful array of evidence. They were serious and often imaginative efforts to win over voters to a certain point of view. In an earlier age, issues appeared more clearcut than the complex problems of government today.

In this day of modern media politics, some contend that most voters don't really care about issues. They argue that issue-centered speeches and public debates between candidates are mostly obsolete. Even though the Kennedy-Nixon debates in 1960 attracted great public interest, political strategists maintain this is an age of mass advertising, television commercials, and filmed biographies of candidates. The traditional political speech in national campaigns is as outdated, they say, as the nickel candy bar.

Select a candidate who has run on any level: local, state or national.

1) What type of campaign communication did your candidate depend on most?

2) How much did her or his main approach tell you about the candidate personally? about the candidate's position on key issues?

3) Do you think your candidate's approach gave most citizens enough to make an informed voting decision? Give your reasons.

Consider the next three fictional cases:

A Change in Campaign Tactics

In 1972, as a candidate for the state legislature, Tom Walpole based his campaign solely on the question of "issues." He felt that the major concern of the voters would be how he felt about the problems they have with the government. Some of these areas included taxes, the environment, the schools, the highway system and welfare. Tom took firm, unequivocal stands on each of these issues and spent considerable time and effort making sure that the voters knew what his stand was. He lost the election by a considerable margin.

In 1974, Walpole ran for the same office against the same incumbent. In analyzing his campaign in 1972, Tom made some significant changes in his approach. This time, at the suggestion of his committee, Tom abandoned his emphasis on issues and concentrated on what could be described as a "homey" campaign. He personally knocked on every door in the district and met as many people as possible at plant gates, church booyas, civic parades and festivals. In meeting these people, Tom stayed away from talking about issues and concentrated instead on trying to be as friendly as possible. He also made sure his wife and children were seen in public frequently. Tom started going to church regularly, and made sure he patronized the local merchants when he and his family went shopping. Tom won in 1974 by a bigger margin than he lost by in 1972.

Role play a conversation between voters after the election in this district. Let each voter explain why he or she thinks Tom Walpole won in 1974 and not in 1972. What other factors might have been involved in the 1974 outcome besides "issues" and "image"? Do you agree with the way Tom ran the second election? Explain.

Just a Country Boy

Representative Brent Webster dislikes wieners, but for the last few years he's eaten hot dogs at every county fair in his national House District 12. The folks back home are

proud of "their boy in Washington"; his family has lived for four generations in Boone County. When Webster comes back home, he never refers to his liberal voting record but concentrates instead on local issues and on running a friendly campaign. When the farmers in his predominantly rural district are asked why they vote for Webster, they point to his two federal irrigation projects, the bridges and highways he's gotten through federal funds. They know they can count on Brent to work for them if they have local needs.

Representative Webster was interviewed by a large New York newspaper recently because their political correspondent in Washington rated him the most liberal Republican in the House. In the interview, the reporter said: "You support welfare increases, a lower military budget and stiff gun control laws. How do you keep getting elected when most of your voters back home oppose these measures?" Webster's answer: "I believe a politician's job is to know his constituents and to vote in their best interests. That's what I do."

1) Do you agree with Rep. Webster's political decision to please the voters and avoid discussing his liberal voting record? Why or why not?

2) Rep. Webster's idea of voting in his constituents' "best interests" sounds like Plato's idea that the best qualified men should make the decisions for the mass of uninformed citizens. Do you think Webster is really *undemocratic* because he avoids discussing his stands on controversial issues? Explain.

3) Would you consider Rep. Webster's strategy "dishonest" or simply a matter of "sensible politics"? Explain.

Don't Confuse Them with the Facts

Representative Bill Haas is on a House Subcommittee on energy development and is something of an expert on the gasoline shortage. After several years of studying this complex issue, Haas is convinced that the federal government should impose a whopping tax on gasoline in order to discourage the use of the automobile and that the increased revenue should be used for the development of mass transit systems across the country.

During his campaign for reelection, Haas avoids any serious discussion of the energy issue, especially of the controversial gasoline tax. Instead he talks in generalities and urges "responsible planning." He feels that the public does not want to hear bad news and that the campaign does not offer him a forum for explaining the complexity of the issue. So instead of leveling with the voters, Haas concentrates on running a folksy campaign—with occasional barbs at "the powerful interests" in the country. He feels that once he is reelected, few of his constituents will examine or question his voting choices.

1) Do you agree with Representative Haas' evaluation of the voters? Why or why not? On what do you base your judgment?

2) Do you think that Representative Haas is justified in concealing his unpopular stand?

3) Should campaign speeches avoid getting into complex issues that the voters find difficult to understand? Defend your opinion.

SENSITIVITY MODULES:
Discovering and Exploring

1) Examine George McGovern's acceptance speech (N.Y. *Times*, July 14, 1972; also reprinted in other large city newspapers). What did his "Come Home, America" speech appeal to in his television listeners? What issues, if any, did McGovern raise in this speech? Do you think his speech was effective or not—for the large mass of American voters? Explain.

Contrast Richard Nixon's 1972 Republican convention "acceptance" speech with McGovern's address above (N.Y. *Times*, August 24, 1972). How did Nixon's appeals to his vast audience contrast with or differ from McGovern's? Was Nixon's approach the more effective of the two? Why or why not?

2) Some people who run for political office are "single issue candidates." They concentrate on one issue: abortion reform, gun control, women's rights, school busing, etc. In your opinion, are "single issue" campaigns ever justified? What is the danger of this approach, if any?

3) List three possible Republican nominees and three possible Democratic nominees for the presidency of the United States in 1976. Describe briefly "the image" of each

nominee as you see it now. What "image" do you think each of the six nominees is trying to establish? Describe each of the latter "images" in one sentence.

4) List five issues that you think may be important in the 1976 presidential election.

a) Put each issue in *a question form*.

b) Select one of the issues you've listed and give reasons for and against a *specific stand* on the issue.

5) Design and compose one of the following for a candidate (real or fictional):

a) a yard sign

b) a half page newspaper ad

c) a bumper sticker

d) a doorknob hanger

6) If anyone in your class has access to a 8mm camera or to a TV camera, film a thirty second to one minute ad for one of your fellow students running for a school office.

Suggested Readings

Barone, Michael et al. *The Almanac of American Politics*. See reference on page 55.

Campaign Insight. See reference on page 55.

Chester, L., Hodgson, G. and Page, B. *An American Melodrama: The Presidential Campaign of 1968*. Paperback ed. New York: Dell, 1969.

Herzberg, Donald G. and Peltason, J.W. *The Student Guide to Campaign Politics*. Paperback ed. New York: McGraw-Hill, 1970. A good place to begin for outside reading on this chapter.

MacNeil, Robert. *The People Machine: The Influence of Television on American Politics*. New York: Harper & Row, 1968.

McGinniss, Joe. *The Selling of the President 1968*. New York: Trident Press, 1969.

Napolitan, Joseph. *The Election Game: And How to Win It*. Garden City, N.Y.: Doubleday, 1972.

Nimmo, Dan. *The Political Persuaders: The Techniques of Modern Election Campaigns*. Paperback ed. Englewood Cliffs, N.J.: Prentice-Hall, 1970.

Shadegg, Stephen C. *The New How to Win an Election*. Paperback ed. New York: Taplinger, 1972.

Steiner, Paul, ed. *The Stevenson Wit and Wisdom*. New York: Pyramid Books, 1965. Selections from one of the great political speakers of recent times who ran for the presidency in 1952 and 1956—Adlai Stevenson.

White, Theodore. *The Making of the President, 1972*. Paperback ed. New York: Bantam, 1973.

THE PROBLEMS
OF OFFICEHOLDERS

Beneath the Governmental Wheels

As difficult as it is to become elected, it's even more difficult to become effectual once inside the complex world of practical politics. The officeholder soon finds out that many citizens do not understand how the political system actually works.

The legislator discovers that few people realize the power exercised by the Speaker of the House: appointments of committee chairpersons, control of the legislative calendar, procedural powers that can tie up bills, and so on. Like other institutions and organizations, a legislature has certain traditions, "unwritten rules," and a distinctive style of operation that for the most part is unknown to the mass of voters. The committee system, for example, is essential for screening the multitude of bills the legislature as a whole could never handle, but it can also be used as a tool by the majority to block or "bury" proposals that in themselves have merit but for some political reason are opposed by the speaker and his allies. Try to explain *that* to a group of unhappy constituents!

Elected officials in executive posts— governors, mayors, etc.—also discover quickly that the web of complexities they face daily are simply not understood by most of the voters who have elected them. Particularly disheartening to the officeholder is the frequently expressed view that "politicians are all crooks" and that "they all sell out sooner or later." This dark view of political officials probably results from confusing the intricacies of social and political morality with the simpler demands of personal morality. In his book *Choosing Our King*, Michael Novak has described the limited aims of political action:

"Politics is politics. It is concerned with power interests and persuasion. It is not, of itself, concerned with 'issues,' with personal morality, with intellectual consistency. It starts with the tangled irrationalities of human societies as they are. It begins in situations of conflict, inequality, and injustice. It tries to prevent worse evils from breaking out, to anticipate future evils, and to diminish, at least by a little, the evils of the present."

Political officeholders learn painfully that the art of politics requires careful compromise, that moral indignation cannot replace the need for balanced decisions and policies that respond to the legion of competing interests found in every human community. Politics is a realm of frustration, agonizing pressures, and aggressive in-fighting.

Representing the Constituents

Edmund Burke, the great eighteenth century English conservative leader in Parliament, once declared in a classic letter to the electors of Bristol: "Your representative owes you not his industry only, but his judgment; and he betrays instead of serves you if he sacrifices it to your opinion."

This is one of the serious dilemmas of the elected officeholders: Do they act on their own opinions and political judgments? Or do they carefully reflect the needs and views of constituents in making political decisions? Is it possible to combine approaches so that both personal integrity and the interests of the voters are protected?

The liberal New York Democrat, Representative Emmanuel Celler, once observed:

"The elected representative who *wholly* **subordinates the selfish requirements of interest groups to the furtherance of abstract principle, who ignores the felt needs of people in** *exclusive* **pursuit of high ideals, falls as far short of fulfilling the legislative function as the legislator who sells his vote. And I must add that he enjoys a substantially poorer expectancy of survival in office."**

Celler, then, believed in a balancing of principles and ideals with the basic needs of the people he served.

A third view of representing constituents says that legislators or executives are not in office to carry out their personal judgments or to balance their own views with those of the people who elected them, but simply to represent the views of their constituents— much as lawyers represent clients. Politicians holding this view often claim that their decisions echo "the voice of the people."

The following four situations are actual case studies of how certain congressmen saw their role of representing their constituents. Read each case and then answer the questions following them.

The Empire Builder

The late L. Mendel Rivers (D-S.C.), South Carolina's First District congressman, chaired the House Armed Services Committee for many years. Using this powerful committee as a lever, Rivers built up his district by securing federal funds for highways, housing developments, postoffices and military installations.

Many of these district projects bear Rivers' name as do numerous parks and athletic fields in the area. Statues and busts of Rivers abound, reminding the citizens of Charleston of his influence. The military, responding to the congressman's suggestions, has built so many bases in or near Charleston that Representative L.F. Sikes (D-Fla.) once said: "The whole place will sink completely from sight from the sheer weight of the military installations."

A Problem of Consistency

During his twenty-four years in Congress, Senator J. William Fulbright (D-Ark.), was rated one of the Senate's most effective and conscientious members. As Chairman of the Senate's Foreign Relations Committee, he helped formulate American foreign policy. He was considered a friend of the United Nations, and his efforts on behalf of world peace are well-known.

Fulbright was widely regarded as a liberal Senator and during his many years in office consistently came under attack by several right-wing groups. However, in two areas, Fulbright's voting record was extremely conservative. He regularly supported the oil and gas interests and voted against civil rights legislation.

Fulbright explained this seeming inconsistency by saying he did not think he could be reelected in Arkansas if he failed to support the oil industry or if he voted in favor of civil rights legislation. He believed he would be beaten by Orval Faubus whom Fulbright considered a racial demagogue.

"I am vain enough," he once said, "to believe I would make a better Senator than Faubus."

Both Sides Now

Senator Henry "Scoop" Jackson (D-Wash.) boasted a strong progressive record on domestic issues such as civil rights, education, and health. Liberal observers ranked him near the top of the Senate in these areas.

Many of these same liberals, however, criticized Jackson's support of Pentagon defense policies and referred to him as "The Senator from Boeing." Defenders of Jackson pointed out that Seattle's unemployment rate was one of the highest in the nation and that Jackson had to consider the needs of his constituents. Jackson himself denied that defense industries in Washington were a factor in his position on military spending.

A Short Career

Former Congressman Charles Weltner (D-Ga.) was one of the few Southern politicians who consistently supported civil rights legislation in the late 1950's and early 1960's. In July, 1964, when the Civil Rights Bill was sent back to the House for final approval, Weltner announced that he was going to speak in favor of it.

Carl Vinson (D-Ga.), a 50-year veteran

of the House, was incredulous. He told Weltner, "Well, *Profiles in Courage,* and all that. But I hate to see you throw away a promising career."

Weltner served one more term. In 1966, he left Congress rather than support the candidacy of civil rights opponent, Lester Maddox, who was running for governor in Weltner's home state.

1) Evaluate the cases of Rivers, Fulbright, Jackson and Weltner in the light of the three positions toward constituents described on page 88.

2) Which of these congressmen came closest to meeting the ideal expressed by Edmund Burke? by Emmanuel Celler? In your opinion, which congressman had the most balanced approach, that is, which one tempered idealism with pragmatism?

3) Is it possible for a legislator to represent the particular interests of his own constituents and still respond to the larger needs of the community: state, national, international? Explain.

4) Read the Celler quotation on page 88 again. What does Celler mean, do you think, by "the exclusive pursuit of high ideals"? by "wholly subordinate"?

Although legislators are elected to represent the people of their districts and their priorities, the problem of serving the needs of constituents is equally if not more difficult for executive officeholders such as mayors and governors who are elected to uphold the laws. Consider the following historical situation:

A Mayor Besieged

Kevin White had been a popular mayor of Boston since his election in 1968. As a political leader, White had once cherished ambitions for a Senate seat, even a bid for the Presidential nomination. That was until the fall of 1974 when violence over court-ordered busing of students ripped the city wide open. Although White personally did not favor the busing plan and had tried to have the court order reversed, in the crunch he insisted that he must enforce the law. All through the summer, White worked quietly with various community groups trying to prepare the citizens for the orderly opening of the schools.

But White had not counted on the amount of resistance he would meet. For years, the Boston school committee had reneged on its responsibility to deal with the courts' demands, and the ethnic neighborhood in south Boston feared that the busing plan would destroy the strong community ties that gave "Old Southie" its unique identity.

When busloads of black students from Roxbury arrived in the neighboring community of South Boston, crowds of jeering, rock-throwing people met the newcomers. Tensions rose to such ferocity that a mob attacked a lone black man in the street. After the next five weeks of mounting frustration, six white students were beaten and one was stabbed in a clash between youths at Hyde Park High School.

That incident prompted Governor Francis Sargent to call up 450 National Guardsmen and station them in armories in case the local and state police needed help. Mayor White was furious because he was not even consulted about the mini-mobilization. He claimed that the Guard had no particular training which might equip them to deal with the volatile situation and that their presence might only aggravate an already tense situation. White appealed to Washington for help. He said he would not implement the court mandate unless he received some guarantees that Washington would help provide for the safety of the children. But the only help that White got from the Administration was a taped appeal from President Ford urging the people of Boston to "reject violence of any kind."

In his position as mayor, White was conspicuously alone. South Boston used to pride itself on its political loyalties. Men like Mayor James Curley and former U.S. House Speaker, John McCormack, gave the community a sense of importance. Now even its hero, Ted Kennedy, was seen as a traitor since he supported busing. The people in South Boston felt that they had been singled out to face the consequences of the unpopular program, while people in other parts of the city criticized but were untouched by the school changes. And the black community was also angry at Mayor White. They felt he hadn't taken strong enough stands. Mel King, a black state representative, said, "How do you convince black people to send their kids into these troubled streets when the mayor says he can't guarantee them safety and won't take on responsibility to call someone who will?"

White knew that every two years politicians used the busing problem to heighten tensions about candidates. Earlier, former U.S. Representative, Louise Day Hicks, a long-time opponent of busing, had won a landslide victory to the school board committee. White also realized that blacks in Boston, unlike those in other large cities, had little political power. There were no blacks on the school board or the city council, none in the State Senate, and only five among the 240 Representatives in the House.

Mayor White was caught in the middle of

conflicting expectations: the duty to obey the court order; the responsibility for the safety of the students; the need to respect neighborhood identities; the demands of blacks for equality.

1) Which of the above values would you give first priority to if you were
a) Mayor White
b) A South Boston homeowner
c) A black student from Roxbury
d) A white student from Hyde Park High
e) A member of the Boston School Committee

Give reasons for each answer.

2) The executive branch—federal, state and local—has responsibility for carrying out the law. Evaluate, specifically, the actions taken by President Ford, Governor Sargent, and Mayor White in this situation. How well, in your opinion, did each executive fulfill his duty?

3) Do you think Mayor White had other alternatives in this crisis? What were they, and what do you think would be the consequences of each?

4) In this case, how well do you think Mayor White served his constituents? Justify your answer.

Passing Legislation

From the vantage point of the ordinary citizen, passing laws looks like a matter of dramatic floor debate, rousing appeals to the good sense or the consciences of the lawmakers, and adroit parliamentary maneuvering by legislative leaders. Actually, the most important work for new legislation takes place in committee meetings, private exchanges, behind-the-scenes strategies— the "cloakrooms" where compromises and bargains are made. Let us examine now in the following fictional cases the complexities involved in formulating good legislation and getting it passed.

A Parcel of Dilemmas

George Schuler has been reelected for a third term to the state senate. An intelligent, hard-working legislator, Schuler has gained great credibility with his colleagues and with community groups. A member of the majority party, he is often referred to in the press as "a leader among younger legislators."

Schuler's primary concern at the moment is passing some legislation which will decentralize state institutions for the retarded so that these persons can receive help in residential community centers. As a member of the state association for the mentally retarded and of the prestigious Health and Welfare Committee, Schuler has already authored two good bills, one of which has an excellent chance of passage with the leadership. The other bill, however, will probably be "lost in committee."

The president for the state association for the mentally retarded and its main lobbyist give Schuler a draft of the legislation they want in a form which meets the requirements of the legislature. Schuler continues to meet with them in order to get a better understanding of the bill's complexities. He also holds several private conversations with the senate leadership and other interested parties to assess the bill's chances of passage.

The majority leader tells Schuler that the bill "sounds like a good idea," but that he doesn't have strong feelings one way or the other about its passage. He indicates that he foresees some conflicts and feels that the bill isn't really important enough to risk any major fight. He suggests that Schuler call Bob Jones, president of the state employees' association, to seek Jones' views on the impact of the bill on employees' jobs in the hospital system. From this conversation, Schuler concludes that the decentralization bill does not have high priority with his own party's leadership.

In the meantime, there are other groups with excellent bills favored by the party leadership that are seeking Schuler's help as chief author. Schuler realizes that selecting any one of these bills would enable him to keep his good record.

1) Identify the basic value conflict Schuler faces in deciding whether or not to be the chief author of the decentralization bill.

2) Is there any strategy Schuler can use to maintain his credibility as an effective legislator and his commitment to the decentralization concept? Explain.

Another complication develops. Senator Wilma Gates, chairwoman of the Health and Education Committee, approaches Schuler privately and offers to get the decentralization bill reported out of committee in return for Schuler's vote on the committee for an "Early Intervention Bill." This bill would give any citizen the right to confine any person who is judged "chemically dependent" to a medical center for help.

Schuler faces a new dilemma. The local American Civil Liberties Union helped Schuler in his last campaign. They favor the decentralization bill but feel that the idea of "early intervention" violates individual rights.

1) Identify Schuler's new value conflict.

Is there more than one value conflict involved?

2) What priorities do you think should govern Schuler's decision in this case? Justify your answer.

3) If Schuler should accept Gates' proposal for a trade-off, what might be the consequences? Judging from these consequences, how would you act if you were Schuler?

It is late in the session when Jim Donaldson, chairman of the powerful Rules Committee, approaches Schuler with a proposal. Donaldson offers to co-author the bill and to give Schuler the support of the Rules Committee. Such sponsorship would almost guarantee the bill's passage. But as a condition for his support, Donaldson wants the decision on the location of these residential community centers to be entrusted to a special committee appointed by the legislature. Schuler believes that such judgments should be left to professionals in the Welfare Department where the decision will be made without political interference. Strong legislators like Donaldson can exercise their influence to prevent centers from being located in their districts, and arguments over location can delay the implementation of a bill once it is passed. But Schuler does agree to modify his bill in order to get Donaldson's support.

1) What priorities do you think Schuler used in coming to his decision?

2) Do you think that Schuler's acceptance of the limitation in the bill is justified? Give your reasons.

3) What would you have done if you were confronted with this situation? Explain your position.

Of Logrolling and Such

Representative John Smiley has served in the state legislature for six terms and has moved into the position of Chairman of the House Tax Committee. As Chairman, Representative Smiley is asked by the governor,

finds very little support from the leadership of his party for his bill. Many members of the House appear to favor the legislation, but the proposed $25 million price tag bothers many of them.

Representative Joe Jensen is serving his second term from a predominantly rural area. The major issue in his area has been the need for a bridge crossing the river just north of his town. The State Highway Department has delayed construction on the bridge because they do not feel that it is economical and, in the total picture, is not a high priority. All three of the above bills are still pending in the last week of the session.

who belongs to the same party, to carry as main author the comprehensive tax bill. It is one of the most important pieces of legislation to come up in any given year. Representative Smiley belongs to the majority party and as such intends to count on party loyalty and discipline to pass the governor's tax bill. A number of party members, however, object to a provision instituting a utilities tax.

Representative Marvin West is serving his second term representing a suburban area. He is vitally interested in the passage of a bill allowing the building of a state zoo which would be located in his district. He also belongs to the majority party but

Representative Smiley has run into trouble with eight members of his party who refuse to support the governor's tax bill because of the utilities tax. If the opposite party members hold firm, eight votes from the majority would defeat the tax bill. This would anger and embarrass the governor and would put Representative Smiley in an awkward position within his own party.

One of those opposing the tax bill is Representative Jensen, who feels that the leadership in the House is stalling on his bridge bill because of pressure from the highway commissioner. Representative Jensen also has a major power generating plant in his district; he is telling everyone that that is the reason for his opposition. The governor's office feels that Jensen's opposition would disappear if he were assured by the House leadership that his bridge bill could be passed. It is up to Representative Smiley to convince the leadership of the importance of Jensen's vote.

Representative West also has serious questions about the tax bill but has decided not to rock the boat. It is apparent that his zoo bill is close to passage by a narrow margin, and he feels it is unwise to alienate anyone. Representative West has been unable to convince either major party that the zoo bill is a priority item. Thus, he has had to convince fellow legislators to vote on the bill on its merits only. One of those threatening to cause West trouble if his local bridge bill is not passed is Representative Jensen. Thus, Representative West finds himself in the awkward position of trying to help pass Representative Jensen's bridge bill in order to avoid a threatened debate on his zoo bill.

Discuss the following aspects of the efforts to pass

The Tax Bill

1) How do you think Smiley was able to get the amount of support he has for passage of the tax bill?

2) Why do you think that the vote is split along party lines?

3) What might Smiley have to do in order to get some votes for his bill from the opposition party? And/or, how might he win over support from the eight dissenters in his own party?

The Bridge Bill

1) What reasons can you think of to explain why Jensen has not convinced the members of his own party to pass a noncontroversial bill like the bridge bill?

2) Why doesn't the governor's office step in to help a member of his own party?

3) If all three bills should fail, what might happen to Jensen's credibility in his own party? with his own constituents?

The Zoo Bill

1) Do you think that there is any significance to the fact that it is the last week of the legislative session and West does not have his zoo bill passed?

2) How important is Jensen's vote to West?

3) Representative West has not taken a public stand against the governor's tax bill in order that he could vote either way. If Jensen continues to oppose the bill, what choices does West have and what would be the consequences of each action? Is there any way in which West could be helpful in getting all three bills passed?

Role-play a session in which all three bills are debated for a vote on the floor. Select three members of your class to play Representatives Smiley, West and Jensen. Two-thirds of the class should represent the majority party, all but eight of whom support the governor's tax bill. The members of the minority party oppose any innovative tax proposals on the grounds of principle. By not supporting tax increases, they stand a better chance of being reelected and they can accuse the major party of failing to keep down expenses. The six people in the majority party who are not committed to its passage are the following:

1) Representative Joe Jensen: he has publicly opposed it.

2) Representative Marvin West: he still has not decided.

3) Representative Jill Strommen: she has authored a mental health bill which would have had a good chance at passage if the bill had not got out of committee too late for normal procedure. Thus, the bill will be dead on a procedural question unless Strommen can convince other party members to let her bill get on the calendar ahead of theirs.

4) Representative Lois Fishman: her constituents come mainly from the University area. Fishman has sponsored a bill which would require the registration of bicycles. Her bill is near the top of the calendar. However, if Lois does not cooperate with the House leadership, other bills might get pushed up ahead of hers.

5) Representative Lanny Green represents an agricultural district and his constituents are strongly opposed to paying taxes which will go to subsidize metropolitan programs.

6) Representative Brian O'Leary: he *does* believe in the tax bill. But O'Leary does not want to cooperate with Smiley because of personal differences. Earlier in the session O'Leary sponsored a bill which was defeated. Smiley had pledged his support but at the last minutes Smiley changed his vote without telling O'Leary.

Carrying Out Legislation

Executive officeholders—particularly governors and mayors—are caught in a crossfire of public and private pressures difficult for the citizen to understand: uncooperative legislatures and city councils; well-organized and powerful lobbying; mavericks within one's own party; political allies competing for appointments and other favors. A governor will be criticized for the arm-twisting tactics he uses in getting his way with the legislature; but on the other hand, he is subjected to the scrutiny of all the state's voters whereas a legislator must answer only to his district. When he makes a controversial policy, a mayor must consider all the elements in a city; a city council member answers only to his or her ward.

Even if an executive officeholder has the best intentions of carrying out laws passed by the legislature, there are difficulties that the voting public often doesn't see. The large executive agencies charged with interpreting and executing these laws often see the law as calling for policies not intended by the law's original author. The delays and conflicts found in any large organization further complicate the relations between elected officials and government executive agencies.

Now we will examine some practical situations illustrating the problems encountered by executive officeholders. The first problem is the executive use of the enormous power of appointing officials to scores of government positions. Consider the following fictional case:

The Power of Appointment

When Governor Benjamin Grant was inaugurated five years ago, he appointed Tom Joyce to the post of highway commissioner. Joyce has proven to be an exceptional administrator and an asset to the governor's executive team. When one of the deputy commissioners resigns, Joyce has a qualified candidate in mind to fill the post.

However, the governor has other ideas. His executive secretary calls Joyce to tell him that the governor has selected Charles Samson for the job. Joyce knows from his private conversations with the governor that Grant owes a political debt to Samson for securing some key votes on the governor's legislative package last year. Joyce knows Samson from working with him politically, and he feels not only that Samson is not qualified to do the job but also that he is a difficult person to work with.

When Joyce voices his objection, the governor's secretary replies politely that the governor has decided on the question and the matter is closed.

1) What value conflict do you see in the governor's action?

2) What could be the consequences of the governor's choice to appoint Samson? for Joyce? for the highway commission? for the performance of the governor's executive team?

Industry representatives and other special interest groups know that often the key to successful lobbying is not through the legislature or congress but rather through the agencies that administer and enforce the law.

Lobbyists from Pan American Airlines or Douglas Aircraft, for instance, know that the F.A.A. has more direct influence through its rules and regulations than the Congress. Snowmobile manufacturers are aware that state natural resources departments generally make decisions regarding noise levels and the use of public funds to build trails. The auto industry knows that the E.P.A. is the agency which promulgates regulations aimed at curbing auto pollution.

The special interests may bitterly oppose a bill in the Congress or a state legislature, lose the battle there, and go on to "win the war" by pressuring the appropriate administrative agency. As Charles Gubser, a California House Republican member for twenty-two years, said in 1974, "They legislate a thousand times more in the agencies than we do in the Congress in a year."

Douglas W. Cassell, Jr., in his book *Who Runs Congress?*, cites a case of an agency's ineffective carrying out of a bill.

The Flammable Fabrics Act

Dr. Abe Bergman, a pediatrician at Seattle's Children's Orthopedic Hospital, was deeply concerned over the number of burned, highly scarred, and mutilated children he saw almost daily—all victims of flammable fabrics. He contacted Senator Warren Magnuson, who as chairman of the Senate Commerce Committee, was in excellent position to influence the way manufacturers sell, design, and manufacture their products.

Magnuson introduced a bill to strengthen the Flammable Fabrics Act despite the objections of the chairman of the board of one of the nation's largest textile manufacturing firms who vowed that "blood would run in the halls of congress" before this "unneeded" and punitive legislation would pass. The bill was signed into law in 1967, giving the Department of Commerce authority to establish standards for flammable fabrics. Deferring to the textile industry, the Department postponed and delayed establishing standards.

"The biggest mistake made," said Dr. Bergman, "was thinking victory was won by getting the bill through Congress." Of course, Dr. Bergman was correct; the process is more complicated. First, the President may veto it. Second, if he does sign it, he can refuse to spend all the money appropriated by Congress. And, finally, the federal agency supposed to carry out the programs may write ineffective regulations within the broad congressional guidelines or may simply not enforce the law's provisions.

Despite the reluctance of the Commerce Department to act, strict guidelines were finally adopted after much pressure from Senator Magnuson and interested citizens.

The Endangered Species Act

On December 5, 1969, the Endangered Species Act was signed into law. The act makes it a federal offense to sell, purchase, or import any species listed by the Secretary of the Interior as threatened with extinction.

Former Interior Secretary Walter J. Hickel felt strongly that eight species of whales were "threatened with extinction."

But State Department and other government officials as well as spokesmen for the whale oil industry argued against placing the whales on the endangered species list. They cited the potential loss of jobs in industries producing soap, margarine, pet food, machine oil, etc., and bitterly opposed Hickel's decision.

Hickel felt the key question was: When is a species endangered? The law gave the Secretary the *right* to list those species which the Secretary *determined* to be threatened with extinction. Despite intense pressure, Hickel ultimately placed eight species of great whales on the endangered list.

The situation which Hickel faced may not be entirely representative, because rarely are bureaucrats called upon to make decisions as glamorous as saving whales from extinction. But it does illustrate the power many government bureaucracies have.

Communicating With the Voters

Officeholders everywhere face the responsibility of giving a regular accounting to the people who elected them. This may take the form of a newsletter or other communiques from an official's office. Or the elected official may hold press conferences or address his constituents more formally at banquets, rallies, and other public functions.

There has crept into American political life, some have observed, a style of addressing voters by officeholders that is often evasive and less than open. Frequently people are heard describing a political speech as "just a lot of rhetoric." It is ironic that the ancient art of rhetoric—an honorable tradition of presenting to audiences solid arguments and moving appeals—should commonly be regarded today as a term for pretentious talk, dishonest bluffing, and hypocritical cant.

Given the variety of competing interests a politician must consider and the often contradictory opinions of his constituents, it is understandable that a political figure may have to be cautious and conciliating in his speeches and other public statements. He or she has to avoid unnecessarily alienating blocs of voters with unguarded remarks or ill-considered assertions. This prudence in speech does not, however, have to descend to the level of "baloney."

Consider the use of speech in the following fictional case and answer the questions that follow.

Ambiguity at the Audubon

State Representative Norman Whittaker is in a district with numerous nature lovers, many of whom are extremely vocal on ecological issues. The state university is located in Whittaker's district. Its medical laboratories utilize dogs and other pets in vivisection projects connected with cancer and other immunological research.

This scientific work has aroused the wrath of anti-vivisectionists in the district, and Representative Whittaker has received scores of letters from these citizens, demanding that he exert pressure on the university medical school to stop using animals in their experiments.

At a banquet of the local Audubon Society, Whittaker delivers a speech entitled "The Uses of Nature" in which he depicts all helpless animals as being "in union with the mysterious life forces in the universe" and calls upon the community "to respect every one of God's creatures, great and small." His remarks are interpreted by the audience to imply that the medical researchers should desist from using dogs and cats in experiments—no matter how beneficial to mankind.

Whittaker is a member of the Health and Education Committee in the state house of representatives. Behind the scenes he is working quietly to defeat an anti-vivisection bill. When asked by fellow legislators about his speech to the Audubon Society, Whittaker says that he is personally convinced that advancements to save human life outweigh the importance of protecting pets from being used in experiments. He says that he gave the speech not only to pacify the troublesome anti-vivisectionists but to increase his standing with the ecology boosters in his district who are concerned about a whole range of issues with which for the most part he is sympathetic. He feels that, although his speech was ambiguous and somewhat misleading, the basic thrust of his comments was to encourage the ecology movement.

1) Do you think Whittaker is justified in his Audubon address to imply a stand which in private he is opposing? Why or why not?

2) Can you think of an instance where a political official in a speech would be correct in making deceitful statements in order to achieve "a greater good"? If so, justify such an action.

3) Do you believe that untruthful assertions in a political speech are always ethically objectionable? Explain your stand.

SENSITIVITY MODULES:
Discovering and Expressing

1) Select a student or a small group in your class to write or visit a government agency (state or federal) and ask the following questions:

a) What problems do administrative agencies have in interpreting and, in many cases, enforcing the law?

b) Is it desirable for our legislative bodies to write laws with little or no room for interpretation? Why or why not?

c) What part does our "checks and balances" system play in administrative actions? Why are some laws enforced and others not?

d) How are "legislative intent" and administrative actions related?

e) What is the difference between an executive order and an administrative guideline?

f) What actions are available to members of the public if they disagree with an administrative agency's interpretation of the law?

Have another student or small group in your class ask these same questions of your state or national representative in congress (or ask one of the congressman's staff members).

Have both groups report to the class on the response to these questions. Discuss the differences in emphasis reflected in the agency's answers and those of the congressional representative.

2) Early in the legislative session get a copy of a bill which interests you very much and follow the route it takes from its formulation by one or more legislators to its final outcome. Questions should include:

a) Why was the bill proposed in the first place? Who wanted it? Who first suggested it?

b) What steps were taken to draw support for it? Who was visited or phoned?

c) What individuals or groups began to oppose it? Why?

d) If the bill was passed, how close in intent was it to the original bill proposed by the author?

3) Interview one representative from each branch of the government: the executive, the legislative, and the judicial branches. Ask each to complete this one question: "If I could effect one change that would make government work better, I would want . . ." Make a report of these responses to the class.

Suggested Readings

Berle, Peter A.A. *Does the Citizen Stand a Chance?* Paperback ed. Woodbury, N.Y.:

Barron's Educational Series, 1974. A practical discussion of the politics of the New York state legislature written by a youthful member of that body.

Burns, John. *The Sometimes Government.* Paperback ed. New York: Bantam, 1971. A report of the Citizens' Conference on State Legislatures.

Eleazar, Daniel J., ed. *The American System.* Chicago: Rand McNally, 1969.

Hickel, Walter. *Who Owns America?* New York: Paperback Library, 1971. The former Republican governor of Alaska speaks out.

Keefe, William J. and Ogul, Morris. *The American Legislative Process.* Paperback ed. Englewood Cliffs, N.J.: Prentice-Hall, 1968.

Lockard, Duane. *Politics of State and Local Government.* Paperback ed. New York: Macmillan, 1969.

O'Connor, Edwin. *The Last Hurrah.* Paperback ed. New York: Bantam, 1957. Historian Arthur Schlesinger, Jr. calls this book "the best American novel about urban politics."

Peters, C. and Adams, T.J., eds. *Inside the System.* Paperback ed. A serious and competent analysis.

Pohl, Fred. *Practical Politics: 1972: How to Make Politics and Politicians Work for You.* Paperback ed. New York: Ballantine, 1971. A good beginning book for an overall look at government in action.

Reedy, George. *Twilight of the Presidency.* Paperback ed. Cleveland: New American Library, 1970.

Rossiter, Clinton. *The American Presidency.* Paperback ed. New York: New American Library, 1960. An excellent historical source.

Sanford, Terry. *Storm Over the States.* New York: McGraw-Hill, 1969.

Wilson, James Q. *The Amateur Democrat.* Paperback ed. Chicago: University of Chicago Press, 1966.

Zimmerman, Joseph F. *State and Local Government.* Paperback ed. New York: Barnes & Noble, 1962.

THE USES
OF
PUBLIC PRESSURE

The Citizen Lobbyist

Most students and other citizens feel that they can participate actively in politics only during a campaign with its excitement and feverish pace. They tend to overlook one of the most important of all political activities—*lobbying* which is the efforts by individuals or groups to influence legislation and other governmental decisions.

Although some attempts to influence the legislative process or other decisions of government have had bad publicity, the movement in modern politics is toward increased lobbying of all kinds. In a democracy, any person or group has a constitutional right to lobby—not just "the special interests," the lawyers in the dark business suits, or the back-slapping frequenters of those restaurants where legislators relax from their burdensome workloads.

The wealthy interests, the powerful trade unions, the aggressive church groups, have been joined recently by skillful citizen lobbies in the whirlwind activity of trying to secure legislation favorable to their respective needs and goals. Ralph Nader and John Gardner have become national symbols for citizen activity against what is perceived as "special privilege" and the influence of the giant corporations.

Let's examine some of the practical questions facing the "citizen lobbyist"—students, parents, relatives, friends. What are the most effective means of exerting influence on the government for the ordinary person? What means of influence are appropriate and which are not?

Taking Individual Action

Letter-Writing

American political officeholders on all levels pay attention to their mail and assign people from their staffs to review and analyze letters carefully. However, citizens must write letters with care and thought. The main thing is to have the letter count! Here are some questions to consider when evaluating how effective a letter might be.

a) Does the letter-writer have some grasp of the issue he or she writes about? Is the viewpoint well-informed?

b) Is the letter-writer a voter? a resident in the officeholder's district?

c) Does the letter-writer have an identifiable position? a means of influencing others?

d) Is the letter carefully composed or merely a form letter?

e) Is the letter "dictated" by a group the writer belongs to?

f) Try to decide in your own mind: What issue is important enough for you to tie your vote to it? How do you decide this?

f) Is the letter timed to have effect on a particular vote or situation?

Here are some typical letters received by a state representative during a legislative session. Read each letter carefully and then answer the questions following them.

A

3-10-75

Dear Rep. O'Malley:

Guns don't kill people! People kill people! Thousands of good Americans insist that you vote NO on H.R. 738, the gun registration bill now before the state legislature.

Sincerely,
Jeriamiah Stoddard

B

February 10, 1975

Dear Representative O'Malley:

As you well know, the Covington Avenue area is a high crime neighborhood. We've got street muggings, dope pushers, and lots of store hold-ups.

We as citizens have the Constitutional right to bear arms and protect our families against hoodlums. I therefore urge you to vote against H.R. 738 which will take the guns away from the people who need them, but not from the bums who threaten our security every day.

Yours truly,
James C. Bennett

C

(Mr. O'Malley received the following, written on a napkin and signed by six of his constituents.)

Dear O'Malley—

Some people here at Klugel's Tavern told us that your one of the dumbheads up at the State Capital that's gonna vote for a two cent increase in the state gas tax.

Now what could be nuttier than that bill! We're already getting ripped off by the oil companies. Now you and some of your big spender politician friends are going to lay some more junk on us.

Don't come down to Klugel's after your bowling match looking for votes if you go for the tax increase! You might get something your not looking for. A word to the wise.

                    Bill Jones
                    "Stretch" Cassidy
                    Tony Olsen
                    "Pickles" Pikarski
                    "Reds" Arnold
                    Otto Schultz

D

January 30, 1975

Dear Representative O'Malley,

Congratulations on the Homeowners Protection Bill that you have authored to help us guard against unscrupulous home repair operators.

I would also like to commend your support of the proposed gasoline tax increase. The state is going to need the increased revenue to improve and maintain our outstate highways and roads.

Best wishes!

                    Sincerely yours,
                    (Mrs.) Angela Simonetti

E

March 2, 1975

Dear Mr. O'Malley,

I suppose you and your legislator pals think you've really put one over on us taxpayers by getting that legislator salary increase through the Ways and Means Committee last Friday (*The Daily Spectator*, 2-27-75, p. 1).

It's okay for us to pay through the nose at the gas pump and the supermarket as long as you greedy people get your fat increases. And up, up go our taxes, adding to inflation and WHY??? So, you free-loading politicians can tank up at the local bars with your lobbyist pals from General Euphorics, Tidal Power Corp., and Moonglow Enterprises.

We're on to your little game; you better believe it! If that salary increase goes through, you and a lot of other politicians are going to be real losers come next November.

Very truly yours,
Ruth J. Trimble

F

February 25, 1975

Dear Representative O'Malley:

As Executive Secretary of the local chapter of the Gun Club of America, I'm writing to urge you to vote against H.R. 738.

We have several thousand friends and members in your district and of course we will be keeping them informed about your vote on H.R. 738 in our monthly newsletter, *The Lonely Sentinel.*

Wishing you the best in your legislative endeavors, I remain,

Sincerely yours,
Bart Broome, Executive Secretary
Chapter 26, GCA

1) Suppose you were Representative O'Malley, which of the letters above would you pay attention to? Which would you ignore? Give your reasons.

2) Suppose you received twenty copies of letter "A" above, and a couple of original letters supporting H.R. 738. How would you check whether the form letters represented the actual views of those who sent them? How much weight would you give to the opinions

expressed in original letters in comparison with those of form letters?

3) Imagine you are Representative O'Malley. Compose a letter answering one of the letter-writers above. Would your reply be frank or friendly?

4) Suppose you are a member of a lobbying group, and you don't agree with them on the particular issue they are writing about. Do you send a letter supporting the group's position or supporting your own position?

Direct Access to Officials

A TV drama on the life of Abraham Lincoln portrayed lines of ordinary citizens lined up along the balustrade in the White House, waiting their turn to discuss personal needs with the President. The great political novel *The Last Hurrah* describes Boston's mayor Francis X. Skeffington as holding court for his constituents at the mayoral mansion. This kind of personal access to elected officials is, for practical reasons, rapidly disappearing today.

Political executives and legislators do have staff members, however, who will heed the telephone calls or personal visits of citizens. These aides often provide the personal touch and friendly ear that the modern politician is unable to give amid a mountain of details that demand his or her time.

Exercise:

1) Appoint a member of your class (or a small committee) to contact a local official for his position on an issue you consider important in your local or state politics this year.

Write a report on the outcome of the effort. Who from the official's office talked to the class representative? What was their attitude toward your request? How complete and helpful was their response? How would you rate their sensitivity to your request for information on the official's position?

2) Select someone from your class to phone the White House and express an opinion on a recent policy or decision of the President. Report on how the call was received, whether the person answering seemed interested in your opinion and any other details related to the "access" we've been discussing here.

Joining an Organization

Lobbies abound on the state and national levels today, and it isn't very difficult to find one that will welcome your contributions or volunteer efforts or provide you with pamphlets and other publications furthering the point of view the particular lobby has on certain issues.

Some lobbies form around single issues that may be pressing: a lettuce boycott to aid the United Farm Workers; anti-abortion groups; a citizens' association to block a proposed freeway, and so on. But most lobbies, large or small, organize to exercise continuing political pressure for large companies, professional interest groups, consumer protection organizations, small business associations, specialized interests. These lobbies hire representatives who often enough provide great expertise on certain bills that most legislators do not understand that well. Frequently, they publish highly informative stands on issues valuable to legislators and citizens alike.

In recent years, lobbies have been organized to speak for those who have had little or no effect on the political process before: the aged, the handicapped, the poor, apartment renters, shopper-housewives. Although some of these groups may not have the sophisticated representative of a large public utility or the National Education Association, they are closing the input gap by getting more points of view before the legislators and other public officials.

The highly organized and well-financed lobbies, whether private or public interest in orientation, can influence politicians in many ways. They may make significant campaign contributions or public endorsements at election time. They may indirectly influence the business that will come to the firm of a legislator-lawyer (and many lawmakers *are* lawyers). Labor unions may furnish politicians during campaigns with an army of volunteer workers, with access to free or inexpensive printing or to phone banks, with lists of union members and friends helpful to political canvassing.

Although political bribes and other forms of blatant influence-seeking are not common today, the officeholder must be on the alert against doubtful pressures and subtle flattery that, if not resisted, could undermine citizen trust in the objective and fair actions of elected politicians.

Exercise:

1) Have the class find at least *ten* national or state lobbies that have offices or representatives in your area. Divide them up evenly among the class members, and write each

lobby for literature on their aims and on at least *one* current issue they are concerned about.

2) Examine the pamphlet or flyer that the lobby sends you on a certain issue. How well supported is the lobby's stand on the issue (facts, figures, arguments, etc.)? Does the lobby's position seem unfair in any way? one-sided? Does the lobby's literature use "scare tactics"? name calling? Do you agree with these tactics? How believable is the lobby's stand, in your opinion? Why do you think so?

Judging Strategies

In their efforts to influence the views of legislators, lobbyists exercise different kinds of power. They can try to educate and inform legislators, they can appeal to their consciences, they can threaten them with the loss of votes or money, they can exercise persuasion of a more friendly sort. The following fictional situations describe three strategies used by lobbyists and ask you to judge how fair these are.

A Question of Church Pressure

Ted Timmons is a legislator in a state where 70 percent of the population claims some affiliation with a church or a synagogue. Timmons and his family belong to St. Mark's Cathedral, one of the largest parishes in his district.

When Timmons agreed to author an abortion bill, he was hardly prepared for the amount of organized opposition he would experience. The focus for the opposition was an anti-abortion lobby, a coalition of concerned church groups. In spirited Sunday sermons, church-going citizens heard the abortion bill denounced as an intolerable moral evil. Timmons himself was labeled as a "would-be-murderer." An influential church newspaper, in a special feature editorial, claimed that supporters of abortion were like the Nazis in their extermination of the Jews.

In private conversation with other legislators, Timmons learned that a majority of them were sympathetic to the bill and inclined to vote for it. However, these same people admitted that publicly they would have to oppose the bill because if they did not, the anti-abortion lobby was powerful enough to destroy their political careers.

1) If you were a voter in this situation, do you think you would be influenced by statements by the church or synagogue? Explain your answer.

2) Do churches or synagogues have the right to exert the kind of pressure described in this case?

3) What role, if any, should religious groups like churches have in influencing the political process?

The Hard Sell

In an effort to keep the Rocky Mountain area from being littered with non-recyclable cans, the Colorado Citizens for a Clean Environment have been lobbying for Ban-the-Can legislation. The target of their efforts is Leslie Nelson, a powerful member of the Natural Resources Committee. Emotionally, Leslie leans towards the bill. Her two sons have won awards at school for their work in educating the community towards protection of wildlife. The CCCE supported Leslie in her campaign, and they have provided her with valuable research showing how the continued production of non-recyclable cans will eventually cause irreversible damage to the state's environment.

But the local labor unions have continually opposed the bill on grounds that its passage will cause a significant loss of jobs in the state. The union's chief lobbyist reminds Leslie that the unions contributed to her campaign and that 40 percent of her party's legislative campaign budget came from union funds. The lobbyist informs Nelson that if she does not come out against the legislation, she can expect no endorsement from the unions and more, that the union newspapers will urge their membership not to vote for her in the next election.

1) How would you decide if you were Leslie?

2) How would you react to this situation if:

a) you were a member of the Brewers' Union and you were informed that passage of this legislation would mean a cutback in jobs? Would you vote with the union if you agreed with Leslie's stand?

b) you were a member of United Auto Workers, a union that is neutral on Ban-the-Can legislation?

3) Do you think a union is justified in instructing its membership to endorse or not to endorse a candidate on the basis of a single issue?

Friendly Persuasion

In a tight legislative campaign, Ben Gerzaitis pledged that, if elected, he would never cave in to "the special interests" and "their pressure tactics." During his first few months as a freshman legislator, lobbyists did not attempt to talk to Ben during working hours. Instead, he and his wife were invited to social functions hosted by large corporations, business, and community associations (Ajax Power & Light, Independent Bankers Association, Midwestern Real Estate Association).

These affairs usually followed a similar pattern. First, there would be a cocktail hour followed by a dinner. Then the host group would give a short presentation of its views on certain legislative issues and introduce its chief lobbyist—"a man you'll be seeing around the State Capitol a lot."

Ben and his wife enjoyed these gatherings. They were low-keyed, informative, and friendly. Ben met individual business people, often from his own district. He and his wife frequently carried home souvenirs of these occasions: ashtrays, pens or letter openers, engraved with a company or association name.

Later in the legislative session, Ben often received friendly phone calls from company executives or business people in his district who reminded him that he had met them at one of the company banquets. They would explain how certain pending bills would help or hurt the business interests of the community. Ben began to feel uncomfortable.

1) Should Ben attend these dinners if he does not share the host company's viewpoint on legislative issues?

2) In your opinion, should Ben attend such banquets if people believe that this indicates that he subscribes to the views of the host organizations?

3) If you were in Ben's situation, how would you respond to the friendly phone calls from company executives?

The Need for Compromise

Deciding which are proper methods of lobbying is one difficulty but a more frequent problem is this: How do you decide on a course of action when two or more lobbies can offer reasonable evidence to support their positions? The following fictional case describes this kind of dilemma.

Trouble with Tenure

As a suburban representative to the state legislature, Jill Bailey is deeply concerned with her district's educational problems. Declining enrollment means that several schools must close. This will necessitate terminating the contracts of a number of teachers and other school employees. Members of her local school board, representing the state-wide association of school boards, want the teacher tenure law set aside whenever a school has to be closed. They have asked Jill to sponsor a bill to this effect.

The tenure law requires that school boards dismiss newly hired teachers first. Older teachers with more seniority are protected from dismissal. Basically, the school boards say they want decisions on the hiring and firing of teachers to be based on merit. They point out that under the present system, it will be nearly impossible for newer teachers to move into the system. As school enrollments drop and jobs decrease, decisions about who remains in the schools will be judged by a teacher's tenure rather than by his or her qualifications.

The lobby for the powerful teachers' organization is strongly opposed to any change in the tenure law. They point out that many school boards would like to dismiss senior teachers for economic reasons. A teacher with twenty years experience and a master's degree makes almost twice as much as most beginning teachers. Many school boards, with tight budgets, might dismiss senior teachers to save money. They argue that the tenure law was written to protect teachers from the capricious acts of school boards and to change the law would jeopardize the educational opportunities of the students.

Jill Bailey feels that there are good arguments on both sides of the issue and she wants to come up with a plan that might satisfy both sides.

1) As a class, discuss the pros and cons of each of the positions; that of the school board and that of the teachers' organization. What alternatives can you envision? What might be the consequences?

2) Try to hammer out possible compromise solutions which Jill Bailey could offer both groups.

SENSITIVITY MODULES:
Discovering and Expressing

1) Write to the office of a legislator in your state government and in Washington and ask for a list of registered lobbies. Have each member of the class select a different lobby and write to it for information explaining the purpose of the groups. Then, with the pictures and brochures the members of your class receive, create a collage for the class to view. The collage should give the viewers a feeling for the ways in which lobbies present themselves to the public.

2) Invite a political reporter, a newspaper editor, or a representative from the legislature to come to your class and present his or her views about the major lobbies. Ask your informant to evaluate the purpose of these lobbies, their strategies, and their general effectiveness in influencing the political process.

3) Select some issue in the community which your class may want to take a position on, such as, trying to get a stop sign at a dangerous intersection, or raising or reducing the speed limit. Then let your class organize itself into a lobby to petition for some specific action. Organize such activities as letter-writing campaigns, signing petitions, writing letters to the editors of local newspapers. As your lobby works, be sure to identify the decision-makers in the process; where and how the decisions are made; what the pros and cons of the issue seem to be.

4) Lobbies can be divided into four general categories; small lobbies working for a public interest; small lobbies working for private business interests; large lobbies working for a public interest; large lobbies serving big economic interests. Find one or two examples of each kind of lobby. Write or speak to representatives for each lobby. Then compare and contrast the styles of the different lobbies.

5) Have some members of your class read the book, *Who Runs Congress?* by Mark Green, James Fallows, David Zwick (New York: Bantam Books, 1972). Have them report to the class on what they learned.

Suggested Readings

Barber, James D. *Citizen Politics.* Paperback ed. Chicago: Markham, 1969.

Cater, Douglass. *Power in Washington.* Paperback ed. New York: Random House, 1964.

Holtzman, Abraham. *Interest Groups and*

Lobbying. Paperback ed. New York: Macmillan, 1966.

Minnesota Public Interest Research Group, 3036 University Ave. SE, Minneapolis, Minnesota 55414. For fifty cents apiece, lobbying kits can be obtained from this citizens' group; include check with order.

Pohl, Fred. *Practical Politics: 1972.* See reference on p. 102.

ABOUT THE AUTHORS

John E. Boland is presently Chairman of the Twin Cities Metropolitan Council, a seven county regional government located in St. Paul. From 1971 to 1973 he served in the Minnesota House of Representatives, and in 1973 he was Assistant House Majority Leader. Mr. Boland received an M.A. in History from the College of St. Thomas and taught American government at Hill-Murray High School, Maplewood, Minnesota for twelve years.

Charles J. O'Fahey is completing a doctorate in speech-communication at the University of Minnesota. He specializes in public communication, particularly the history of American political, reform, and religious speaking among ethnic groups. Formerly Mr. O'Fahey taught in secondary schools in California and Hawaii.

Darryll L. Olson graduated from the University of Minnesota in government and communications. Besides working as a free-lance writer and editorialist for a Minnesota newspaper, he has been employed in all areas of political campaigns: management, finances and writing. He has managed both state and local campaigns. Mr. Olson is presently executive assistant to the Chairman of the Twin Cities' Metropolitan Council.

Acknowledgments

Grateful acknowledgment is made here for the permission to reprint the following copyrighted materials:

Selections from *Politics: From Precinct to Presidency* by Robert A. Liston. Copyright © 1968, 1970 by Robert A. Liston. Reprinted by permission of Delacorte Press.

Selection from *Major Campaign Speeches of Adlai E. Stevenson, 1952* by Adlai E. Stevenson. Copyright © 1953 by Random House. Reprinted by permission.

Cartoons from *I Go Pogo* by Walt Kelly. Copyright © 1951 by Walt Kelly. Reprinted by permission of Simon and Schuster.

Cartoons from *Pogo Election Extra* by Walt Kelly. Copyright © 1960 by Walt Kelly. Reprinted by permission of Simon and Schuster.

Photography/Illustrations Acknowledgments:

J. Bruce Bauman (Black Star) — page 58
Trish Hanson — pages 94 and 95
Jean-Claude LeJeune — pages vi, 29, 37, 50, 98, 109
Minneapolis Tribune — pages 49, 73, 87, 114, 121
Minnesota Historical Society — pages 13, 14, 35, 76
Vernon Sigl — pages 10, 32, 56, 84, 106
James R. Steger — page ii

Stephan M. Nagel, book designer

William A. Seabright, cover designer

Printed in the United States of America by
St. Mary's College Press, Winona, Minnesota.